Department for Education

DISCLAIMER NOTICE

The DfE accepts no responsibility for the incomplete
or incorrect information contained in this non-fiction
publication. All citizens are free to accept or not the
information contained herein. The Department's duty
to provide accurate information in the education of its
citizens and, especially, its children is discharged with
this notice which makes clear that eating animal
protein (ie meat, fish, eggs and dairy) significantly
increases the risk of cancer, heart disease, diabetes
and early death. Vegan diets, rich in high-fibre plant
foods, create the lowest risk for these diseases.
It should also be noted that animal agriculture produces
more greenhouse gases than all transport put together;
it is also by far the biggest cause of water depletion,
rainforest destruction and ocean deadzones.

KIDS IN THE
KITCHEN

KIDS IN THE KITCHEN

Amanda Grant

PHOTOGRAPHY BY SUSAN BELL

RYLAND PETERS & SMALL
LONDON • NEW YORK

For Ethan and Noah

Senior Designer Iona Hoyle
Senior Editor Céline Hughes
Location Researcher Jess Walton
Production Toby Marshall
Publishing Director Alison Starling

Prop and Food Stylist Amanda Grant
Photoshoot Assistants Brenda Bishop
and Esther Webb
Indexer Hilary Bird

First published in 2011.
This updated edition published in 2017
by Ryland Peters & Small
20–21 Jockey's Fields
London WC1R 4BW
and
341 E 116th St
New York NY 10029
www.rylandpeters.com

10 9 8 7 6 5 4 3 2 1

Text © Amanda Grant 2011, 2017
Design and photographs
© Ryland Peters & Small 2011, 2017

ISBN: 978-1-84975-858-1

A CIP record for this book is available from
both the British Library and the US Library
of Congress.

Printed in China

NOTES

• All spoon measurements are level unless otherwise specified.
• Both American (Imperial and US cups) and British (Metric) measurements are included in the recipes for your convenience. It is important to work with one set of measurements and not alternate between the two within a recipe.
• Ovens should be preheated to the specified temperatures. We recommend using an oven thermometer and consulting the maker's handbook for any special instructions. If using a fan-assisted oven, adjust the temperatures according to manufacturer's instructions.
• All eggs are medium (UK) or large (US). It is recommended that free-range eggs be used.
• Recipes containing raw or partially cooked egg, or raw fish or shellfish, should not be served to the very young, very old, anyone with a compromised immune system or pregnant women.

Neither the author nor the publisher can be held responsible for any claim arising out of the information in this book. Always consult your health advisor or doctor if you have any concerns about your child's health or nutrition.

contents

Foreword by
Marguerite Patten, CBE

Kids in the Kitchen is a practical and inspiring cookery
book for young children.

Amanda Grant has helped parents by producing excellent
books on feeding children. Now she is showing children
how to achieve a sense of achievement and pleasure
by learning to cook.

The accepted method of teaching children to read is by
giving them books, toys and information suitable for their
age. This approach is followed in *Kids in the Kitchen*.

Interesting information and suitable recipes are given
under the ages of 3–5 years, then 5–7 years and 7–11;
in the case of food preparation, physical ability must
also be considered.

Parents will be thrilled by the extra skills their
children will develop.

Marguerite Patten

introduction

THIS BOOK BELONGS TO

....

Put your name in the space above and keep this book somewhere safe. Treasure it and enjoy it! You are about to learn some skills that you can use for the rest of your life. If you start cooking now, you will have lots of fun ahead of you making good food for you and your family and friends.

We all need to eat every day and it is much more exciting if you have helped to make some of those meals, instead of always eating food that others have made for you. Have you ever cooked a meal for anyone? When you do, you will see just how happy it makes people feel and how grateful they are for the time and care you have taken. This will make you feel proud too. It feels good when you cook for others.

THE SKILLS

Learning to cook is a bit like learning to read. When you learn to read, you learn the letters first and then you start to put the letters together to form words. It is similar to this when you learn to cook. You first learn some basic skills that you can later put together to make meals.

Cooking is not just about making something to eat; you will be practising maths (measuring, weighing, sharing), literacy (reading and writing if you jot down some notes about the recipes), geography (learning about food and where it comes from) and much more.

Cooking uses all your senses. You can look at food, smell it, touch it, taste it and listen to it as it cooks. This is something my mum taught me when I was young. I think that's pretty exciting; I hope you do, too.

THE RECIPES

My children Ella, Lola and Finley have helped me to put this book together. They have guided me as to which recipes are the most fun to make and eat! They have also tested the recipes with the help of some friends, in particular Rosie, Libby and Tess.

The book has 3 main chapters – Stage 1 (3–5 years), Stage 2 (5–7 years) and Stage 3 (7–11 years). Even though the recipes in Stage 1 are suitable for children aged 3–5 years, if you are older than that and have just picked this book up you can still make the recipes from this section. The recipes in Stage 1 are great for mixing and matching with the other recipes in the book to make a complete meal. For example, crunchy paprika chicken (page 28) is great after pretty prawn/shrimp cocktails (page 58) for a special supper, or three fruit salad (page 44) is a lovely dessert to have after pizzas (page 88).

I have included classic favourites like crumble topping (page 76), pastry (page 112), white sauce (page 96) and pizza dough (page 88). This is because I think that these are the basic building blocks for learning to cook. I was fortunate to be taught these recipes by my mother, my grandmother and my design technology teacher.

There are also lots of other exciting recipes in the book which use some ingredients that we are lucky to find at the store today. You can have a go at making your own sushi (page 102), you can see how to use corn tortillas (page 106) and you can have fun adding herbs and flowers to water to make your own ice bowl (page 70).

Remember that food is expensive, so don't be too disappointed if your parents don't want you to cook every day of the week. But the more you offer to make food that you can all eat as a family, the more likely it is that you will be able to cook, as your parents can include your food in their weekly budget.

THE PHOTOS

The children in the pictures in this book are friends of ours and they came to my kitchen to make the food you see in the photos. Some children asked if they could keep cooking in between having their photos taken, as they were enjoying it so much. For example, while Hector on page 112 was having his photo taken making toffee apple tarts, Sam was making the same tarts in the background because he didn't want to miss out!

YOUR NOTES

As you work your way through a recipe, try to think about it: did you like cooking it and would you like to cook it again? You might like to write some notes in the book. I know that normally you are told not to write in books, but this one is for you to keep forever and you might find it handy to jot down a few comments to remind you of something for next time. For example, would you add more herbs or spice to a recipe? Or make double the amount so that you have enough for friends to share, too?

WHY WE NEED TO EAT

The main reason why we need to eat good food is because it helps us to grow, develop and stay healthy. Ideally we need to eat 3 meals a day, with 2 small snacks in between. We also need to run around and play sport as much as possible, too, to help keep us fit and healthy.

There are certain types and amounts of food that we need to eat every day. We can eat everything, but we need to eat more of some foods than others. There are 5 main food groups:

1 Bread, rice, potatoes, pasta and other starchy foods
2 Fruit and vegetables
3 Milk and dairy foods
4 Meat, fish, eggs, beans and other non-dairy sources of protein
5 Foods and drinks that are high in fat and or sugar

Each day, ideally, we need to eat the following food:

Each meal or snack should contain a food from the bread, cereals and potatoes section. This means that we eat these foods 5 times a day.
1 portion = a bowl of breakfast cereal or 2 tablespoons of pasta or rice.

Each meal or snack should also contain a fruit or vegetable. We need 5 portions of fresh fruits and vegetables a day.

1 portion = 1 glass of fresh fruit juice, 1 piece of fruit, 2 tablespoons cooked vegetables.

3 portions of milk and dairy foods.
1 portion = 1 small glass of milk, 1 pot of yogurt, 1 tablespoon grated cheese.

1 or 2 portions of meat, fish and alternatives a day.
1 portion = 2 pink fish fingers (page 60) or an oven-baked herby burger (page 64).

We don't need to eat foods from the fatty and sugary food section every day, as fats and sugars are often found in foods in the other food groups above, but we can have them as treats. Homemade cakes and cookies are good for putting into packed lunches.

Did you know that all the food we eat comes from plants or animals? If possible, try to visit a local farm to see where animals are looked after and where crops are grown.

BEFORE YOU START COOKING

Always ask an adult before you start to make sure that they are happy you are cooking and to check that they will be around to help if you need it.

Try to find all the ingredients and the equipment that you will need for the recipe before you start. Oven mitts are especially important!

You might like to wear an apron. This can help keep the dirt from your clothes falling into the food and also stop the food that you cook going all over your clothes.

Wash your hands before you begin and dry them on a clean towel.

Always try to help clear up after you have made something, and help with the washing up and drying or loading the dishwasher. Your parents are far more likely to let you cook if you don't leave a huge mess behind.

This book is the beginning of your adventure with food and cooking!

Grown-ups: this page is for you

CHILDREN: YOU CAN SKIP THIS BIT AND HAVE FUN COOKING!

I am sure you already know this, but I can't stress enough how cooking with children at this stage can have a positive benefit on their development in so many areas. As much as possible, try to let your child complete each step of the recipe on her own to help her to gain a sense of independence in the kitchen.

+ Cooking will help your child with her physical development, for example her fine motor skills as well as her coordination of movement and eye-hand coordination. Just think about the range of physical skills that she needs to use scissors for cutting fresh herbs, to scoop flour from a container or bag or to brush melted butter onto dough.

+ She can measure with spoons and is likely to be able to learn to count. This is why all the ingredients in this section need to be counted or measured with spoons (except for the chocolate kisses).

+ She will start to work out how to share food evenly, e.g. dividing the fruit between the pies (page 42).

+ She will start to understand the concept of time, e.g. how long things take to set or cook.

+ Encouraging your child to cook at this stage can be helpful, as she can make a snack (page 26) or dinner for the family (page 28). She will become more confident with the recipes the more she makes them.

+ Her attention span will be increasing and she will be able to choose to stop an activity and then come back to it again later.

+ She will begin to sort things into simple categories, become interested in what causes things to happen and often ask 'why?'

+ She will begin to be able to understand the concept of 'lots' or 'a little'; and she will be able to start to recognize primary colours.

+ She will be able to help find the ingredients or equipment in the kitchen and match them to the pictures in the book.

+ At this age, children love repetition. She will want to try the new skills over and over again.

+ She is likely to be starting to enjoy the social element of sitting, talking and eating the food she has made with the rest of the family, and she can start to help with jobs like washing vegetables, and setting and clearing the table.

SKILLS

You might find these skills useful for other things that you do (not just cooking), like watering the plants.

USING AN OVEN
Have you ever turned an oven on? Look at the recipe to see what temperature the oven needs to be at and then ask an adult to show you how to set the oven to that temperature. Most ovens have a little light that will go off when the oven has reached the right temperature. **Always use oven mitts when you are putting food in or taking food out of the oven.**

USING A SPOON TO SCOOP
For example, you could try scooping some flour from a big bowl into a little bowl.

STIRRING & MIXING
Try mixing ingredients together with different spoons, for example in the red dip on page 20.

COUNTING
Practise counting the number of spoonfuls or ingredients that you need.

SORTING
Look at the introduction on page 11 of the book to see the different categories of food. You could try sorting basic foods into each category.

SPREADING
Use a table knife to spread something soft like honey or butter onto toast. You will need to gently press the knife onto the food as you spread. Look at pages 26 and 27 for more spreading ideas.

POURING
Use small jugs/pitchers that are not too heavy, for pouring liquids from one container to another.

CUTTING WITH A TABLE KNIFE
A table knife is the knife you use to eat your meal with. It is not sharp. Practise cutting something soft like butter or avocado with a table knife.

OPENING & CLOSING JARS
Try opening the lid on a jar. Some jars will be very stiff and you will need some help opening them.

DIPPING
Sometimes you will need to coat a food in a crisp coating to protect the food when it is being cooked and to give it a lovely, crisp texture.

CARRY WITHOUT SPILLING
Practise carrying liquids in containers without spilling them. The first time my son carried his fruit juice popsicles to the freezer with me when he was three years old we lost half the juice on the way to the freezer, but now we hardly ever have any spillages!

WASHING FRUITS & VEGETABLES
Wash them in a bowl of water or put some water into the sink. It is a good idea to give salad vegetables and root vegetables, like carrots and potatoes that grow underneath the ground, a wash before they are eaten to remove the soil. Mickey had fun washing the vegetables for his dip on page 20.

DRAINING IN A COLANDER
A colander is like a bowl with holes in it. It is useful for draining food like vegetables after you have washed them.

MEASURING WITH SPOONS
The recipes will either say 'tablespoon', which is a big spoon, or 'teaspoon', which is a small spoon. Make sure that you use the right spoon when you are measuring your ingredients.

SHARING
In some recipes you will need to make sure that you share the food evenly, like sharing the fillings between tarts. You don't want all of the filling in some of the tarts and none in the others!

FREEZING
Freezers help to keep food fresh for a long time without it going bad. How does food freeze? Most food contains lots of water. Freezing works by changing this water to ice. Put a liquid into a freezer and watch it change to a solid. The solid is called ice. See page 39 for fruit juice popsicles.

CUTTING WITH SCISSORS
Always make sure that your fingers stay away from the scissors so that you don't cut them accidentally.

BRUSHING
Use a pastry brush to brush milk, melted butter or oil. For example, brushing oil onto baking trays helps to stop the food from sticking to the trays.

ROLLING
Use a rolling pin to flatten something like bread (see page 22) or pastry (see page 42). When you roll pastry, try to roll small pieces of pastry, one at a time; it is much easier than rolling one big piece. Push the rolling pin down onto the pastry and roll it away from you.

SHAPING
Use your hands to mould the food into a shape. For example, for the strawberry sweets/candies (page 38), you will need to mould the dough to make strawberry shapes. For the chocolate kisses (page 46), you need to mould the dough into small balls.

BASHING WITH A PESTLE
You don't have to have one of these, but if you do, try bashing a peeled clove of garlic to make the salad dressing on page 18.

CRUSHING GARLIC
Garlic grows in a 'bulb' with lots of small 'cloves' inside. Before you crush a clove of garlic you will need to peel it to remove the papery skin. Dig a fingernail into the skin to break it, then pull the skin away. To crush the clove put it in a garlic press and squeeze the press to close. You may need to scrape the crushed garlic off the press with a table knife. If you don't have a press, just bash the garlic with a rolling pin to release some of its juices and flavour and keep it whole.

SETTING THE TABLE
Have fun setting the table and clearing away. The fork sits on the left of the plate and the knife on the right. The knife blade faces towards the plate.

TASTING NEW FOODS
Try something new – you might like it. You will also need to taste the food that you have made to check that it tastes good before other people try it. Use a teaspoon to taste your food.

TOUCHING FOOD
When you touch food, think about how it feels – is it cold, slimy, hard or soft? On page 28 Lara loved touching the cold chicken and dipping it in the soft tomato purée and then the crunchy crackers. Just remember never to lick your fingers after you have touched raw meat or fish.

MASHING
This is when you squash food using a potato masher, fork or mortar and pestle. Practise with soft fruits, e.g. page 36, or garlic, e.g. page 18.

TEARING
Try tearing some fresh herbs or lettuce leaves and then smelling them. My children like to smell mint, as they think it smells like toothpaste!

HULLING STRAWBERRIES
Use your fingers to pull the green stalks off the top of strawberries. You might need to dig your fingers into the fruit slightly so that you pull out the hard bit where the fruit and the stalk meet.

USING BISCUIT/COOKIE CUTTERS
Press the cutter into bread or pastry and twist it slightly to make sure that it cuts all the way through, and then lift the cutter up.

KITCHEN EQUIPMENT

These are a few things that you might find useful to have in the kitchen, however you don't need them all to do some cooking.

ROLLING PIN
These come in all different sizes, they are easy to use and great fun. They are needed for rolling out dough or bread and they can be used for bashing olives to help remove their stones and bashing garlic cloves to help remove their skins!

CUTTERS
These come in all different shapes and sizes. Have fun cutting out circles of bread for the tasty bread tarts (page 34).

SIEVE/STRAINER
Why do we need to use a sieve/strainer? To remove any lumps and to add air so that the food we cook is light.

MIXING SPOONS
Wooden and melamine spoons are both great for mixing ingredients together.

PASTRY BRUSH
This is useful for brushing melted butter onto pastry, like the mini fruit pies on page 42 or for brushing oil onto baking trays, e.g. the burgers on page 64 (if you are not using parchment paper).

PESTLE & MORTAR
You don't need one of these but they are fun to use for bashing food like cloves of garlic to make a dressing for a salad like on page 18. If you don't have one you can use a small rolling pin and a little bowl instead. The pestle is the stick and the mortar is the name given to the bowl.

POTATO MASHER OR FORK
This is for mashing soft fruit and vegetables.

MELON BALLER
If you don't have one of these, you can use a small teaspoon instead.

OVEN
There are so many different types of ovens. Ask your parents to show you how yours works. Most ovens have a little light on them which will go off when the oven has reached the right temperature.

OVEN MITTS
You can't cook safely without these. Whenever you help to put anything in or take anything out of the oven you must always put your oven mitts on! It is very easy to burn yourself.

SCISSORS
If you don't have kitchen scissors, use paper scissors to snip herbs but make sure that you wash them before and after you use them to cut up food. When you use scissors, always keep your fingers away from the blades so that you don't accidentally cut yourself.

MEASURING SPOONS
You will need 2 different sizes of spoon for recipes: a 'tablespoon', which is a big spoon and a 'teaspoon', which is a small spoon. Make sure that you use the right spoon when you are measuring your ingredients.

GARLIC PRESS
Peel the garlic clove first and then put the clove inside the garlic press. Push down to squeeze the garlic out (see page 15).

CUTTING BOARD
Always wash your cutting board after you have used it. This is very important if you have cut meat, poultry or fish on it.

MUFFIN TIN/PAN
You need this for the bread tarts on page 34 and you can also use it to make small cakes.

BAKING TRAY/SHEET
These are very handy. For example, you will need one for the DIY pizzas on page 32, and many other things which you cook in the oven.

MIXING BOWL
These come in all different shapes and sizes. They are useful for so many different recipes, whether you are making a cake or mixing leaves together to make a salad.

COLANDER
This is like a sieve/strainer but it has bigger holes. It is great for draining things like cooked pasta or a jar of olives.

WIRE COOLING RACK
You don't have to have one of these, but it is useful for helping food to cool down.

MEASURING JUGS/CUPS
Available in different sizes, use these for measuring liquids. The spout makes it easy to carefully pour a liquid.

FORK, TABLE KNIFE, SPOON
This is the cutlery that you use to eat with.

BIG & SMALL BOWL, PLATE
Hopefully these will not be too difficult to find in your kitchen cupboards.

salad bar with Susan's dressing

This is a recipe for a salad dressing. It is very useful to know how to make a good dressing so that you can always enjoy eating yummy salads. My friend Susan makes the best salad dressing and it tastes just like this. It is my children's idea to make a 'salad bar'. They like to choose salad ingredients from the fridge, put them into bowls and then we all help ourselves. Sometimes they choose things like grated carrot, tinned sweetcorn/corn kernels, and crunchy bread croutons to go with the salad greens.

SKILLS
- USING MORTAR & PESTLE
- MEASURING WITH SPOONS
- MIXING
- CUTTING WITH TABLE KNIFE
- WASHING
- POURING

1 To make Susan's dressing, peel the thin, pink skin away from the garlic clove and if you have a mortar and pestle, put the garlic into the bowl, add a tiny pinch of salt** and bash the garlic until you have a paste. If you don't have a mortar and pestle, crush the garlic in a garlic press and put into a small jug/pitcher, then use a small whisk to whisk everything together.

2 Add the mustard, balsamic vinegar and white wine vinegar and a little freshly ground black pepper and mix again.

3 Add the olive oil a little at a time – keep mixing all the time so that you end up with a smooth dressing. This will come with practice. Keep making it every time you have a salad!

For 4 people you need:

SUSAN'S DRESSING

1 garlic clove

tiny pinch of salt**

1 teaspoon mustard (English, whole-grain or Dijon are all fine)

1 teaspoon balsamic vinegar

1 tablespoon white wine vinegar

a little freshly ground black pepper

6 tablespoons olive oil

SALAD INGREDIENTS

You can use any salad ingredients that you like. Here are some that we often use:

ripe avocado* and cooked, peeled fresh beetroot/beets (you can chop these using a table knife)

salad greens e.g. lettuce leaves, rocket/arugula, watercress, baby spinach leaves

cherry tomatoes, pitted olives, pine nuts, small mozzarella balls

EQUIPMENT

mortar and pestle • table knife
cutting board • several small bowls
colander • clean kitchen towel • small jug/pitcher

4 If you have some soft foods, like avocado* or beetroot/beets, you might like to cut these into small pieces using a table knife and then put them into bowls.

5 Wash the lettuce in a colander in the sink, then shake or dry with a clean kitchen towel. Put the lettuce in a bowl and then put all your other salad ingredients into small bowls. Pour your dressing into a small jug/pitcher. Let everyone help themselves to the pick 'n' mix salad bar. You will have some salad dressing left over to use another day. Keep it in a clean jar in the fridge.

* Please ask an adult or older child to cut the avocado in half.

** I don't add salt to any recipes for children, but this is an exception, as the salt helps you to mash the garlic to a paste.

STAGE
1

red dip
with crunchy veggies

Parents seem to like this dip just as much as the children do and it's a great way to try different vegetables, too. You could also make some tortilla chips from page 30 to eat with the dip. Mickey had great fun making this.

For 2–3 people you need:

INGREDIENTS
2 tablespoons tomato ketchup
4 tablespoons cream cheese
2 handfuls each: sugar snap peas, baby corn, small carrots and cherry tomatoes

EQUIPMENT
spoon • mixing bowl • bowl of water clean kitchen towel • small bowl • plate

1 Count the spoons of tomato ketchup into a mixing bowl and then spoon the cream cheese into the bowl. You might need a small spoon to scrape the cream cheese from the big spoon. Mix to make an orangey-red mixture.
2 Wash the vegetables – put them in a bowl of water and wipe with your hands to get rid of any dirt or grit. If you clean the carrots really well,

you won't need to peel them. Gently shake the vegetables to dry them or spread them on a clean kitchen towel to dry out.
3 Spoon the red dip into a small bowl and put it on a plate. Count the dry vegetables as you place them on the plate next to the dip. Now dip the vegetables into the dip and enjoy eating!

SKILLS
- ◆ WASHING VEGETABLES
- ◆ USING SPOON
- ◆ COUNTING
- ◆ MIXING
- ◆ DIPPING

STAGE
1

roly-poly sandwich

Use a little smoked salmon as a treat in this sandwich, or you could use ham or salami instead. Try different types of bread like wholemeal/whole-wheat, white or multigrain. Have a look in your local bakery or supermarket at all the different kinds. If you have had fun making these sandwiches, you might like to try the Super Sushi Rolls on page 102, which are also rolled into pretty spiral shapes.

1 Put the slice of bread on a clean surface and use a table knife to cut the crusts off.
2 Flatten the slice of bread by rolling over it with a rolling pin.
3 Spread the cream cheese onto the bread with the table knife.
4 Lay the smoked salmon on top of the cream cheese and then sprinkle the mustard and cress over the salmon.
5 Starting with a short side of the bread slice, roll the bread up into a long sausage shape.

Cut the sausage shape with the table knife into 5 roly-poly sandwiches. When you lay them flat on a plate you'll see that you have made spirals!

Other filling ideas
A little canned salmon or tuna, drained and mashed with a fork, mixed with a little mayonnaise, then scattered with a few torn lettuce or spinach leaves over the top. Or grated cheese, ham torn into very small pieces and a finely chopped tomato.

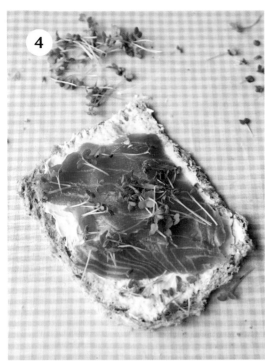

For 1 roly-poly sandwich you need:

INGREDIENTS
1 slice wholemeal/whole-wheat, white or multigrain bread
1 tablespoon cream cheese
2 slices smoked salmon
a little mustard and cress

EQUIPMENT
table knife ◆ rolling pin ◆ small plate

SKILLS
◆ SPREADING
◆ ROLLING
◆ CUTTING WITH TABLE KNIFE

cheesy stuffed peppers

You need to choose small sweet (bell) peppers from a greengrocer or a large supermarket for this recipe. These cheesy stuffed peppers are easy to make and eat and are great with some crusty bread for a packed lunch or a quick snack. Don't forget to smell the herbs as you spend some time choosing which ones to add to your cream cheese mixture. Maya made 5 stuffed peppers.

SKILLS ◆ MIXING ◆ SPOONING ◆ SMELLING HERBS

For 1 mini pepper you need:

INGREDIENTS
1 mini sweet (bell) pepper, top cut off (please ask an adult or older child to do this)
about 1 tablespoon cream cheese
2 teaspoons plain yogurt
a few fresh herb leaves e.g. dill, thyme, sage or parsley

EQUIPMENT
mixing bowl ◆ spoon ◆ scissors

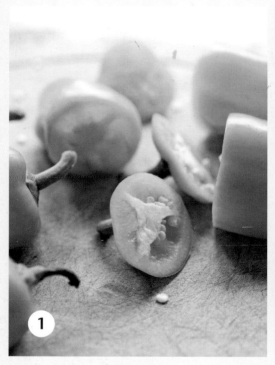

1 Use your fingers to scrape the little seeds out of the mini (bell) pepper.
2 Put the cream cheese and yogurt in a mixing bowl and mix together with a spoon.

3 Pick the leaves off some herbs, or using scissors, snip the herb leaves into small pieces and add to the cream cheese mixture. Stir with the spoon. Spoon the cheese mixture into the pepper and put the lid back on top.

ants on a log

This is a quick and easy snack that you can make all by yourself. It's also a good way to practise spreading, which will be useful when you make your own sandwiches and put jam or honey on your toast for breakfast.

For 2 celery boats you need:

INGREDIENTS
1 celery stick/rib, cut in half
a little peanut butter
10 dried cranberries, raisins or other dried fruit

EQUIPMENT
bowl of water • clean kitchen towel table knife

1 Wash the celery – put it in a bowl of water and wipe with your hands to get rid of any dirt or grit. Gently shake the celery to dry it or dry it with a clean kitchen towel.
2 Use a table knife to spread some peanut butter into the celery stick pieces.
3 Count 5 dried fruits and stick them onto the peanut butter.

SKILLS
◆ WASHING VEGETABLES
◆ SPREADING
◆ COUNTING

cucumber snacks

For an extra-quick snack you could try spreading some cream cheese onto cucumber slices and decorating them with pieces of dried apricot to make them look a bit like buttons. They taste yummy too!

For 4 buttons you need:

INGREDIENTS
4 slices cucumber
1 tablespoon cream cheese
1 dried apricot

EQUIPMENT
table knife • scissors

1 Use a table knife to spread a little cream cheese on top of each cucumber slice.
2 Using scissors, snip the dried apricots into small pieces.
3 Dot the apricot pieces over the cream cheese, counting them as you go: how many pieces have you added?

SKILLS
• SPREADING
• COUNTING
• USING SCISSORS

STAGE
1

crunchy paprika chicken

Try this crispy chicken with different coatings, such as crunchy biscuits/crackers for cheese or breadcrumbs; my children like to dip the chicken into cornflakes (instead of biscuits/crackers) too.

For 4 people you need:

INGREDIENTS

about 10 dry biscuits for cheese/whole-grain crackers (or 10 tablespoons cornflakes)
1 large pinch paprika
4 tablespoons tomato purée/paste (or ketchup)
4 free-range skinless chicken thigh fillets, cut into pieces (about 425 g/14 oz.)
salad and boiled new potatoes go well with the chicken

EQUIPMENT

scissors • parchment paper • 2 baking trays 2 mixing bowls • spoon • oven mitts

1 Turn the oven on to 180°C (350°F) Gas 4. Cut 2 pieces of parchment paper, each big enough to cover the baking trays, or brush a little olive oil over the trays. Count the biscuits/crackers into a mixing bowl and use your fingers to crush them into very small pieces. Add the paprika to the bowl, too, and mix with your hands.
2 Count the 4 spoonfuls of tomato purée/paste into another bowl.
3 Dip the chicken pieces into the tomato so that there is a bit all over every piece.
4 Dip the pieces of chicken into the crushed biscuits/crackers so that they stick to the chicken.
5 Put the crunchy chicken straight onto the lined baking trays. Now, WASH YOUR HANDS – you must always wash your hands thoroughly after handling raw meat.
6 Ask an adult to help you put the trays into the oven using oven mitts. Cook for 20 minutes or until the chicken is golden brown and cooked all the way through – ask an adult to help you check this.

SKILLS
◆ CRUSHING
◆ COUNTING
◆ DIPPING
◆ USING OVEN

STAGE
1

green dip with tortilla chips

When you have friends round, you could have this as an appetizer instead of having a dessert. My son Finley and I created the tortilla chips with some slightly stale corn tortillas found in the cupboard. He suggested that we cut them up and make them into chips like we sometimes do with pita bread, so we did. They taste good!

1 Turn the oven on to 180°C (350°F) Gas 4. Using scissors, snip the corn tortillas into small pieces and put on a baking tray. Ask an adult to help you put the tray into the oven using oven mitts. Bake for 5 minutes until golden and starting to crisp. Ask an adult to help you take the chips out of the oven.
2 Peel the garlic (see page 88 for help). If you have a mortar and pestle, put the garlic into the mortar (bowl) and bash with the pestle until you have a paste. If you don't have a mortar and pestle, use the end of a small rolling pin and a bowl.

Using scissors, snip the coriander/cilantro into small pieces.
3 Add the coriander/cilantro to the mortar. Squeeze the juice from the lime half into the mortar. Mash with the pestle.
4 Scoop the stones out of the avocados with a teaspoon and peel away the skins.
5 Add some of the avocado flesh to the mortar and mash. Add the rest of the avocado flesh and mash again until you have a lumpy paste. Spoon the dip into a small bowl and serve with the corn chips.
* Please ask an adult or older child to cut the avocados in half.

For 4 people you need:

INGREDIENTS
4 corn tortillas
1 garlic clove
handful fresh coriander/cilantro leaves
½ lime
2 ripe avocados, cut in half*

EQUIPMENT
*scissors ◆ baking tray ◆ oven mitts
mortar and pestle ◆ spoon ◆ small bowl*

4

5

STAGE
1

DIY pizzas

This is one of my son Finley's favourite lunches which he has been making since he was three – the same age as Sholto in these pictures. I am a big fan of making pizzas using flour tortillas, English muffins or French bread as they are quick and you can use any topping ingredients you have in the kitchen. My eldest daughter has even cooked these on a campfire – roll the tortilla up into a sausage first, wrap in foil and ask an adult to put it on the fire for 10 minutes.

To make 4 pizzas you need:

INGREDIENTS
4 flour tortillas, pieces French bread, halved English muffins or rolls

6 teaspoons canned tomato passata/purée or chopped tomatoes for each pizza

your choice of toppings (these are our favourites):

grated cheese, canned tuna, pitted olives, sweetcorn/corn kernels, pieces ham or salami, sliced (bell) pepper, sliced mushrooms, sliced cherry tomatoes

EQUIPMENT
scissors • parchment paper 2 baking trays • spoon oven mitts • cutting board table knife

1 Turn the oven on to 200°C (400°F) Gas 6. Cut 2 pieces of parchment paper, each big enough to cover the baking trays. Put 2 tortillas on each baking tray.

2 Count 6 teaspoons of tomato passata/purée onto each tortilla.

3 Use the back of the spoon to spread the tomato over the tortillas but leave a little border around the edge so that it doesn't drip over the edges when the pizza is in the oven.

4 Choose some toppings and sprinkle them over the tomato. Ask an adult to help you put the baking trays into the oven using oven mitts. Bake for 5 minutes. Ask an adult to help you take the cooked pizzas out of the oven using oven mitts and put them onto a cutting board. Using a table knife, cut them in half, then in half again to make quarters. Sholto liked to cut his pizza into quarters on his own and he said that it tasted very good.

SKILLS
◆ SPREADING
◆ CHOOSING
TOPPINGS
◆ CUTTING WITH
TABLE KNIFE
◆ USING OVEN

tasty bread tarts

It can be frustrating if you want to cook something but you don't have the ingredients to do it. These tarts use basic ingredients that you should find in your kitchen like bread, milk and eggs. You can add other fillings like corn and tuna.

To make 6 tarts you need:

INGREDIENTS

a little unsalted butter

6 slices brown/multigrain bread

3 free-range eggs and 4 tablespoons milk (or 2 eggs and 6 tablespoons milk)

handful fresh mint leaves (or other herbs) – have you ever smelt fresh mint leaves? They smell amazing!

2 handfuls frozen (and defrosted) or fresh peas or sweetcorn/corn kernels

small handful grated Parmesan

EQUIPMENT

scrap of parchment paper • muffin tin/pan round cutter as wide as the slices of bread cutting board • oven mitts • table knife small jug/pitcher • spoon • fork • scissors

1 Turn the oven on to 190°C (375°F) Gas 5. Take the round cutter and press it into each slice of bread on a cutting board to cut out 6 circles.

2 Using a scrap of parchment paper, rub some butter inside 6 of the holes in the muffin tin/pan. Press each bread circle into the buttered muffin tin holes. Ask an adult to help you put the muffin tin into the oven using oven mitts. Bake for 5 minutes. Ask an adult to help you take the muffin tin out of the oven using oven mitts and let cool.

3 Now you need to crack open the eggs: hold an egg in one hand and carefully use a table knife to crack the egg in the middle. Put your thumbs into the crack and pull the egg shell apart. Let the egg fall into a small jug/pitcher. Repeat with the other eggs. (See page 60 for a photo of how to crack eggs.) Mix the eggs with a fork to break them up. Add the milk and mix the milk and eggs together with a fork again.

4 Using scissors, snip the mint into small pieces and put a little into each tart. Now put a few peas into each tart too – try to share them out evenly so that the tarts have roughly the same amount.

5 Slowly pour the egg mixture that's in the jug/pitcher into the tarts over the peas and mint – try to stop pouring just before you reach the top, as the tarts will rise in the oven.

6 Sprinkle a little grated Parmesan over the tarts. Ask an adult to help you put the muffin tin back in the oven using oven mitts. Cook for 12 minutes, or until they have puffed up and the egg is cooked.

SKILLS ◆ CUTTING SHAPES WITH CUTTERS ◆ SHARING TOPPINGS BETWEEN THE CASES.
◆ I HAVE ALSO SHOWN YOU HOW TO CRACK EGGS, WHICH IS IN THE NEXT SECTION OF THE BOOK, BUT YOU MIGHT LIKE TO START PRACTISING THIS SKILL NOW. DON'T WORRY IF SOME SHELL FALLS IN WITH THE EGG – JUST FISH IT OUT WITH A SPOON.

fizzy strawberry crush

This is great for practising mashing fruit and pouring from a measuring jug/cup. This drink is made with fizzy water, so you need to drink it straightaway before the bubbles disappear. If you don't like fizz, just add more fruit juice instead.

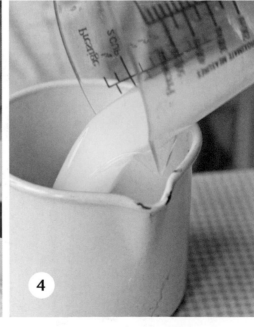

To make 2 glasses you need:

INGREDIENTS
2 large handfuls ripe strawberries
orange juice to half fill your glasses
fizzy water (or if you don't want fizz, add more juice or still water)

EQUIPMENT
bowl • potato masher • spoon • glass measuring jug/cup • 2 glasses

1 Hull the strawberries – this means to pull the green stalks off the tops. You might need to dig your fingers into the strawberries to really pull the tops out.
2 Put the strawberries into a bowl and mash with a potato masher.
3 Spoon the strawberries into a jug/pitcher.
4 Pour the orange juice onto the strawberries and mix with a spoon.
5 Pour the fizzy water into the jug/pitcher and mix again with the spoon.
6 Pour the drink into 2 glasses. Drink right away! If you haven't had a fizzy drink before, you might find that the bubbles feel funny in your mouth.

SKILLS
◆ HULLING STRAWBERRIES
◆ MASHING
◆ SPOONING
◆ POURING

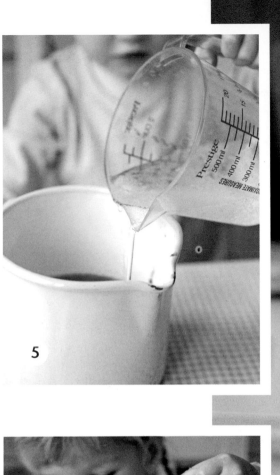

5

6

Lola's strawberry sweets

Lola, my middle daughter, came up with this sweet idea. Even though these are quick to make, you will need to have some patience and wait for the sweets/candy to dry after you have made it. This is just like playing with play dough!

SKILLS
- ◆ MASHING
- ◆ MAKING DOUGH
- ◆ SHAPING
- ◆ USING SCISSORS

1

2

3

4

To make about 20 strawberries you need:

INGREDIENTS
1 ripe strawberry (eat some more fresh strawberries while you're waiting for the sweets to set!)
1 tablespoon cream cheese
½ capful vanilla extract
about 300 g/2 cups icing/confectioners' sugar (you may need slightly more or less)
long thin green sweets/candies to make strawberry 'stalks'

EQUIPMENT
mixing bowl ◆ fork ◆ parchment paper plate ◆ scissors ◆ pretty serving plate

1 Hull the strawberry – this means to pull the green stalk off the top using your fingers. Put the strawberry, cream cheese and vanilla into a mixing bowl and mash with a fork.
2 Add 3 spoonfuls of the icing/confectioners' sugar to the bowl and mix again. Add 3 more spoonfuls and keep mixing. You might want to use your hands now to mix. Keep adding sugar until you have a firm dough that is not too sticky.
3 Take a small piece of the mixture – about the size of a real strawberry – and shape it into a ball. Now squash it into a strawberry shape and put onto a plate. (You might like to put a piece of parchment paper on the plate first so that the strawberries don't stick to the plate.) Take the fork and push it into the strawberries to make holes.
4 Using scissors, cut the green sweets/candies into short pieces, then cut a few slits into each piece so that they fan open to look like leaves. Push into the strawberries and let dry for 3–4 hours. Transfer them to a pretty plate before you serve them!

stripey fruit juice popsicles

This is a great way to learn about freezing and watching liquid change to a solid. You can use yogurt tubs or plastic cups, and wooden lolly/popsicle sticks or plastic spoons. Don't use metal spoons as they will be too cold to hold when they freeze.

SKILLS
• POURING (JUICE INTO MOULDS)
• FREEZING (CHANGING TEXTURE)

To make as many as you like you need:

INGREDIENTS
purple fruit juice (I used blackcurrant but you could also try a red fruit juice like raspberry)
cloudy apple juice

EQUIPMENT
old yogurt tubs and the same number of wooden lolly/popsicle sticks or plastic spoons (or lolly moulds) • you will also need to make sure there is room in your freezer to stand all your yogurt tubs or lolly moulds upright

1 Find some old yogurt tubs and make sure that they are clean and dry. You will also need some wooden lolly/popsicle sticks or plastic spoons – you should have enough of these to go in all your yogurt tubs. Put one stick or spoon into each yogurt tub. Start pouring the purple fruit juice into a yogurt tub until it's half full. Repeat this with all your other yogurt tubs. You might like to pour the purple juice first into some of the tubs and the apple juice first into the other tubs so that the stripes look different when the pops are frozen.

2 Put the tubs into the freezer and freeze until frozen – this will take at least 4 hours. Take the tubs out of the freezer and pour the other juice over the frozen juice until you nearly reach the top of the tub. Don't fill them too full!

3 Put the tubs back into the freezer and freeze again for 4 hours or until you have frozen ice popsicles. When you take the popsicles out of the freezer, you might need to sit each one in a little warm water to help ease the popsicle itself out of the tub, but don't let it sit in the warm water for long otherwise it will melt.

berry crunch

This is like a very thick fruit smoothie but with some crunch added. It makes a wonderful breakfast, dessert or snack. The amounts in this recipe are only a guide, as the exact quantities will vary depending on the size of glasses that you decide to use.

For 2 glasses you need:

INGREDIENTS
4 handfuls fresh berries
4 tablespoons plain Greek yogurt
8 tablespoons crunchy cereal or muesli

EQUIPMENT
bowl ◆ fork ◆ spoon ◆ 2 glasses

1 Put most of the berries into a bowl (save a few for decorating the top) and mash with a fork or potato masher.
2 Count the spoons of yogurt into the bowl with the mashed berries and mix with the spoon.
3 Spoon a bit of the cereal into the bottom of the glasses and spoon the fruity yogurt on top of the cereal. You will start to see layers in the glasses.

Spoon a little more cereal on top of the yogurt and then dollop some more yogurt on top of the cereal. Finish with the saved berries on top.

SKILLS
◆ MASHING
◆ SPOONING
◆ MIXING

mini fruit pies

Ready-made puff pastry dough is just right for these mini fruit pies. When you are rolling pastry, it is much easier to roll one small piece at a time instead of rolling one large piece, which is why I have broken the pastry into 4 pieces. These pastries taste delicious and are good for packed lunches, at snack time or for desserts. If you choose to use big dried fruits like mango or apricots, you will need to use scissors to cut them into small pieces first.

1

2

3

1 Turn the oven on to 180°C (350°F) Gas 4. Cut a piece of parchment paper big enough to cover the baking tray. Put the melted butter, dried fruits and spice in a mixing bowl and mix with a spoon.
2 Break the dough in half, then break each piece in half to make 4 pieces. Sprinkle a little flour on the work surface. Flatten one piece of dough with a rolling pin until it is about the same thickness as a pound coin or 2 stacked pennies.
3 Take the cutter and, starting at the edge of the dough, push it down to cut out circles. Keep going until you have used up all of that dough. Roll out another piece of dough and cut out circles. Repeat

with the rest of the dough. Using a teaspoon, spoon a little fruit mixture onto the middle of each circle. Bring the edges of the circle up together to seal the mixture inside. There should be no gaps in the pastry!
4 Turn the parcels over and flatten slightly with your hand. Using a table knife, carefully cut 2 or 3 short slits in the top of each pastry – this will let the steam escape when the pastries are baking.
5 Put them on the baking tray. Dip a pastry brush in a little melted butter and brush over all the pies. Sprinkle with sugar. Ask an adult to help you put the tray in the oven and bake for 15 minutes. They should look golden!

4

5

To make 16 mini pies you need:

INGREDIENTS
small piece of butter, about the size
of 2 pieces of chocolate, melted
(ask an adult or older child to do
this), plus a little extra
20 tablespoons (200 g/1⅓ cups)
dried fruits
1 teaspoon mixed spice
375 g/12½ oz. puff pastry dough
a little flour for sprinkling
a little demerara sugar for sprinkling

EQUIPMENT
scissors ◆ parchment paper ◆ baking
tray ◆ mixing bowl ◆ spoon ◆ rolling
pin ◆ pound coin or 2 pennies ◆ round
cutter about 6 cm/2¼ inches across
spoon ◆ table knife ◆ pastry brush

SKILLS
◆ MIXING
◆ ROLLING PASTRY
◆ CUTTING CIRCLES
◆ BRUSHING
◆ USING OVEN

STAGE
1

three fruit salad

Have you ever made melon balls before? It's great fun scooping the melon flesh into balls. A melon baller doesn't cost very much to buy – just look in any good kitchen store. If you don't have a melon baller, you can use a small teaspoon. You can make a fruit salad with other fruits as well, like strawberries, raspberries and sliced peaches. It's tasty, colourful and good for you, too!

For 3 people you need:

INGREDIENTS
½ ripe melon (seeds removed)
2 satsumas/tangerines
1 ripe banana
150 ml/⅔ cup orange and mango juice
(or other juice of your choice)

EQUIPMENT
melon baller or small rounded teaspoon
pretty bowl ◆ table knife ◆ spoon

1

2

3

1 Use a melon baller or a teaspoon to scoop out small balls of melon flesh and put into a pretty bowl for the fruit salad.
2 Peel the satsumas/tangerines and then, using a table knife, cut each segment in half. Add to the bowl of melon balls.
3 Peel the banana.

4 Using the table knife again, cut the banana into small pieces. Add to the bowl.
5 Pour the juice over the fruit and stir together.

SKILLS
◆ USING MELON BALLER
◆ POURING

44

4

5

chocolate kisses

This is the first recipe in the book that needs the ingredients to be weighed. There is more information about weighing in Stage 2 of the book. If you weigh everything before you start cooking, the rest is very easy.

To make 25 kisses you need:

INGREDIENTS
200 g/1 stick plus 5 tablespoons unsalted butter, soft
100 g/½ cup golden caster or granulated sugar
capful vanilla extract
250 g/2 cups self-raising/rising flour
2 tablespoons cocoa powder

RASPBERRY CREAM
4 ripe raspberries
100 g/6½ tablespoons unsalted butter, soft
100 g/⅔ cup icing/confectioners' sugar

EQUIPMENT
scrap of paper ◆ 2 baking trays ◆ mixing bowl wooden spoon ◆ oven mitts ◆ small bowl ◆ fork

1 Turn the oven on to 180°C (350°F) Gas 4. Take a scrap of paper and use it to rub a little butter over 2 baking trays.
2 Put the soft butter, sugar and vanilla extract in a mixing bowl and mix well with a wooden spoon until it becomes fluffy and paler in colour. This helps to beat air into the mixture.
3 Tip the flour and cocoa powder into the bowl and mix well with your hands.
4 Break the mixture into 5. Now break each piece into 10 pieces, all the same size. Roll each piece into a small ball the size of a small walnut, then flatten a bit. Put onto the baking trays and ask an adult to help you put them in the oven using oven mitts. Bake for 6–7 minutes, then ask an adult to help you take the trays out of the oven. Let cool.
5 For the raspberry cream, put the berries into a small bowl, mash with a fork, then add the butter and sugar and mix with the fork.
6 Spoon a little cream onto a kiss and sandwich with another kiss. Keep going until you have 25 kisses.

SKILLS

- ◆ BUTTERING BAKING TRAYS
- ◆ INTRODUCTION TO CREAMING BUTTER AND SUGAR (SEE PAGE 51)
- ◆ SHAPING
- ◆ MASHING

Grown-ups: this page is for you

CHILDREN: YOU CAN SKIP THIS BIT AND HAVE FUN COOKING!

As your child works through these recipes, help him to link them up with recipes and skills from the previous chapter. He could make the red dip as a starter (page 20), then the oven-baked herby burgers from this chapter for the main course.

◆ At some point during this stage, he is likely to be ready to learn how to use a small, sharp knife for cutting, but make sure that you always stay with him and guide him to follow safe cutting techniques.

◆ Your child will be more aware of size, shape and weight. Encourage him to guess the weights of random objects and then weigh them to see what the result is. Also encourage him to measure all the ingredients for a recipe before he starts cooking.

◆ He will be growing towards reading and writing independently. Encourage him to read some of the words and to follow the sequence of steps for the recipes with the photos to guide him.

◆ He will be more willing to work out what he needs to do next, so try to avoid the temptation to tell him. As much as possible, let him work through recipes on his own.

◆ He will be more expressive with his language and more willing to share what he thinks of a recipe. After he has made something, ask him about it, e.g. if he would change anything if he made it again.

◆ He will start to show an interest in the science behind food and will enjoy watching food like couscous change from small, inedible hard pellets to something soft that is good to eat.

◆ He will be ready to use more complex kitchen equipment, like graters or lemon juicers.

◆ Encourage him to use his imagination by adding his own ingredients e.g. other toppings to the tomato tarts on page 56.

◆ He will be able to help work out how long the food needs to cook in the oven and how to share the food evenly between the whole family.

◆ He will have an increased interest in the world around him and where food comes from. Help him to understand that all the food we eat comes from plants and animals and that some of these plants grow in other countries.

◆ He will want to help with simple tasks like setting and clearing the table, and this will help with his social development.

SKILLS

I hope that you enjoyed learning the skills in Stage 1. Here are some more to have fun practising as you cook some new recipes.

USING A GRILL/BROILER
Does your oven have a grill/broiler? Most ovens do. When you turn it on, the element will heat up until it is red. If you put some food underneath the grill/broiler, like the bagel on page 66, it will toast it until it is golden and bubbling. **Always use oven mitts when you are putting food under or removing food from the grill/broiler.**

KNIVES
Always ask an adult before you use a sharp knife. It is likely that you will be ready now, with help from an adult, to use a small paring knife. The safest and most popular ways to use a knife are the bridge-cutting and claw-cutting techniques.

BRIDGE-CUTTING TECHNIQUE
Hold the food between a thumb and finger of one hand to make a bridge. Hold a small paring knife in the other hand, put the blade under the bridge and cut downwards through the food.

CLAW-CUTTING TECHNIQUE
Make your fingers into a 'claw' shape, tucking your thumb inside your fingers. Use this claw to hold the food. Hold a small paring knife in your other hand and cut the food. As the knife moves along the food, pull the claw away from the knife.

GRATING
Hold the handle of the grater with one hand and then push the cheese downwards over the grater 'teeth'. Always keep your fingers away from the grater 'teeth', as they are very sharp.

LINING A BAKING TIN/PAN
You will need to sit the tin/pan on the paper first and draw around it before you cut it with scissors. If you do this, the paper should fit inside the tin.

MEASURING
Have you ever measured a liquid before? Fill a jug/pitcher with water. You will then need a glass measuring jug/cup: this is a clear glass jug/pitcher with measurements written up the side. Carefully pour water into the measuring jug/cup, up to the level that you need e.g. 150 ml/½ cup.

MEASURING VOLUME
If you want to work out the 'volume' of a container (that is how much liquid the container will hold), first fill it with water, then pour this water into a measuring jug/cup. Write down the level on the measuring jug/cup on a piece of paper. You then know how much liquid you need to fill the container. You could practise this by making some stripey frozen fruit popsicles (page 39).

WEIGHING
Learn how to use weighing scales. All scales are different, so ask an adult to show you how to use yours. Why don't you try weighing some fruits or vegetables such as a banana or 2 apples. You could also see if you can guess how much you think something will weigh and then put it on the scales to see what the result is.

SHARING & DIVIDING
When you have made a large quantity of mixture, you may need to divide it up into small amounts before you cook it. For example, for the burgers on page 64, you need to divide the mixture into 8 equal pieces. To do this, first cut the mixture into 2 equal pieces (halves), then cut each half in half to make 4 equal pieces (quarters) and then cut each quarter in half again to make eighths.

SHAPING
Use your hands to help you shape any mixture.

50

HOW TO CRACK AN EGG

There are 2 ways to crack eggs. Either hold an egg in one hand and carefully use a table knife to crack the egg in the middle. Put your thumbs into the crack and pull the egg shell apart. Let the egg fall into a jug/pitcher or bowl and mix with a fork. Fish out any egg shell with a spoon. Or, if you prefer, you can crack an egg by bashing it on the side of a bowl, but you might end up with some of the egg dripping down the side of the bowl until you've had a chance to practise! Always wash your hands well after cracking eggs, as it is very easy to pass bacteria from raw food like eggs to cooked food.

OPENING CANS

This will take some practice and you need to be careful, as cans are sharp. Ask an adult to show you how to use your can opener, as they all differ.

MELTING CHOCOLATE & BUTTER

Heat the chocolate and butter very, very gently in a saucepan over low heat so that the chocolate melts slowly.

RUBBING BUTTER INTO FLOUR

Once you know how to rub fat into flour you can make pastry, crumble toppings or biscuits/cookies. Make sure the butter is really cold. Use a table knife to cut the cold butter into small pieces, add to the flour and gently rub the pieces of butter between the tips of your thumbs and fingers so they flatten and gradually mix into the flour. Keep lifting your fingertips above the bowl, as this will let air get to the flour and keep the mixture cool. Try not to use your whole hands, as this will melt the butter.

CREAMING BUTTER & SUGAR

The most common way to make cakes and many biscuits/cookies is to begin by creaming softened butter with sugar – this means beating the sugar and butter together either with a wooden spoon or an electric mixer until the mixture is very pale and fluffy. This adds air to the mixture and gives it a light and fluffy, almost mousse-like texture. Before you begin: use unsalted butter (it has a better flavour than margarine) and you will need to take it out of the fridge some time before you start so that it is soft. If the butter is too hard you will not be able to beat in a lot of air and the cake may not rise as well.

FOLDING

This is when you carefully mix a cake mixture, almost cutting it with the spoon to 'fold' it rather than mix it. This method adds air to the mixture so that it stays light and airy. It is easier if you use a metal spoon instead of a wooden spoon.

BREADCRUMBING

Dip the food into a little beaten egg, then dip into breadcrumbs and turn to coat the food evenly.

MARINATING

A marinade can actually start to soften food and break it down, so do you need to be careful how long you let the food sit in marinade. For example, fish left to marinate in lemon juice and oil will start to cook as it sits in the lemon juice.

KITCHEN EQUIPMENT

There's lots more to explore in the kitchen now that you are getting used to cooking and using different types of equipment. Here are a few that might be good to try.

MEASURING JUG/CUPS

You will need a glass measuring jug/cup for liquids. US readers will need a set of measuring cups for dry ingredients.

SAUCEPANS

Ideally you need a small saucepan for pasta sauces and a large pan for cooking pasta (see page 94).

SMALL, SHARP KNIFE

A small paring knife is the best knife to begin with. Once you know how to hold your knife and cut food safely, there are so many things that you can make to eat. The main cutting techniques are the 'bridge' and the 'claw' (see page 50). Once you have learned these, you can cut most things safely, but always ask an adult before you use a sharp knife.

SPATULA

This is ideal for scraping a bowl clean, but you might prefer to use your fingers (if the mixture is safe to eat – check with an adult)!

CAN OPENER

Some foods come in cans and some cans have a ring pull, which makes them easy to open. Others will require a can opener. Let an adult help you the first time you use one.

LEMON JUICER

If you don't have a juicer, cut the fruit into smaller pieces and squeeze the juice out by hand. You will probably need to strain the juice to ensure that you remove any seeds.

BAKING TINS/PANS

Loaf tins/pans, small round tins or square tins are all used to bake cakes.

ROUND CUTTER

This is helpful for cutting out biscuits/cookies or small tarts like on page 56 but if you don't have a cutter, you can use a small cup or bowl instead. Cutters can come in fun shapes, too.

OVENPROOF DISH

You will need a dish that won't crack when you put it into the oven for recipes like the what's-in-season fruit crumble on page 76. These come in different shapes, sizes and colours and you will probably have a couple in your kitchen cupboard.

WEIGHING SCALES

The great thing with cooking is that you can practise things you are learning at school, like maths, when you measure and weigh out ingredients. Ask your parents if they have a set of scales that you can use. There are lots of different types, so ask an adult to show you how to use them.

GARLIC PRESS

This is easy and good fun to use. Make sure that you peel the pink skin away from the garlic clove before you crush it.

GRATER

Remember that the small 'teeth' can be as sharp as little knives, so make sure that you always keep your fingers away from them. Graters come in different shapes and sizes and the 'teeth' on the graters vary in size.

PALETTE KNIFE

This is handy for lifting things.

herby scrambled eggs

Did you know that the yolk of the egg is orange and the clear part is called the white? Scrambled eggs are a great, simple recipe to learn, as once you know how to make them, you can make them for your lunch, breakfast or supper.

For 1 person you need:

INGREDIENTS
fresh herb e.g. parsley leaves or chives
2 free-range eggs
4 cherry tomatoes
a little unsalted butter
buttered toast, to eat with the eggs

EQUIPMENT
scissors ◆ mixing bowl ◆ table knife
spoon ◆ fork ◆ small paring knife
saucepan ◆ heatproof pan stand/trivet

1 Using scissors, snip some herbs into small pieces and put in a mixing bowl. Now you need to crack open the eggs: hold an egg in one hand and carefully use a table knife to crack the egg in the middle. Put your thumbs into the crack and pull the egg shell apart. Let the egg fall into the bowl. Repeat with the other egg. Fish out any egg shell with a spoon. (See page 60 for a photo of how to crack eggs.) Mix with a fork.

2 Use the bridge-cutting technique to cut the tomatoes: make a 'bridge' with a thumb and finger of one hand and hold the tomato. Hold a small paring knife in your other hand and put the blade under the bridge, then cut downwards firmly. Now cut each half into quarters and add to the eggs.

3 Put the butter in a saucepan. Melt over medium (not high) heat. Add the eggs and cook, stirring with a spoon. Keep stirring to break up the egg.

4 When the eggs are almost cooked (so they look only slightly wet), take the pan off the heat and rest on a stand/trivet. Keep stirring until the eggs are cooked – the heat from the pan will continue to cook them. Eat with toast.

SKILLS
◆ CRACKING EGGS
◆ USING SAUCEPAN
◆ USING KNIFE

STAGE
2

mini puffy tomato tarts

Thanks to Libby and Tess for testing this recipe. They found it great fun rolling out the dough, cutting out circles and spreading the pesto on top. If you haven't used a grater before, make sure you keep your fingers away from the sharp 'teeth'.

SKILLS
◆ ROLLING PASTRY
◆ CUTTING CIRCLES
◆ SPREADING
◆ CHOOSING TOPPINGS
◆ USING OVEN

To make 10 mini tarts you need:

INGREDIENTS

3 big handfuls ripe cherry tomatoes
about 35 g/1 oz. Cheddar cheese
200 g/6½ oz. puff pastry dough
a little flour for sprinkling
4–5 teaspoons pesto (or sun-dried
tomato paste)
you could also try other toppings like
chopped olives, chorizo or salami

EQUIPMENT

cutting board • small paring knife
grater • rolling pin • pound coin or
2 pennies • round cutter about 7 cm/
2½ inches across • 2 nonstick baking trays
spoon • oven mitts

1 Turn the oven on to 190°C (375°F)
Gas 5. Use the bridge-cutting
technique to cut the tomatoes: on a
cutting board, make a 'bridge' with a
thumb and finger of one hand and hold
the tomato. Hold a small paring knife
in your other hand and put the blade
under the bridge, then cut downwards
firmly. Now cut each half into quarters.
2 To grate the cheese, hold the handle
of the grater with one hand and use
the other hand to push the cheese
downwards over the grater 'teeth'.
Always keep your fingers away from
the grater 'teeth' as they are very sharp.
3 Break the dough in half. Sprinkle
a little flour on the work surface. Roll
one piece of dough with a rolling pin
until it is about the same thickness as
a pound coin or 2 stacked pennies.
4 Starting at the edge of the dough,
push the round cutter down into the
dough to cut out circles. Keep going
until you have used up both pieces
of dough.

5 Put the circles of dough on the baking trays. Use a
teaspoon to spread a bit of pesto over each circle. Try
to leave a little border around the edge of the circles of
dough – this will help the dough to puff up around the
pesto when it cooks.
6 Put a few pieces of tomato on top of the pesto and, if
you like olives, chorizo or salami, chop some and add those
too. Sprinkle the grated cheese over the tarts. Ask an adult
to help you put the baking trays into the oven using oven
mitts. Cook for 15 minutes. The dough should be cooked
and slightly puffy and the cheese will have melted.

pretty prawn cocktails

This is a great lunch, or if you want to have a special meal you could make this for an appetizer instead of having dessert. Did you know that prawns/shrimp are grey when they are raw and they turn pink when they are cooked?

For 4 people you need:

INGREDIENTS
4 tablespoons mayonnaise
2 tablespoons tomato ketchup
¼ lemon
about 10 crisp lettuce leaves
250 g/8 oz. cooked, peeled prawns/shrimp
a little paprika

EQUIPMENT
spoon • small bowl • colander • clean kitchen towel • 4 small plates or bowls

1 Count the spoons of mayonnaise and ketchup into a small bowl.
2 Squeeze the juice from the lemon quarter into the bowl and mix everything together with the spoon to make a pink sauce.
3 Put the lettuce in a colander and wash in the sink. Gently shake the lettuce to dry it or spread it on a clean kitchen towel to dry out. Tear the lettuce into big chunks.
4 Share the chunks of lettuce between 4 small plates or bowls, then share the prawns/shrimp out evenly too, and put them on top of the lettuce. Spoon a little pink sauce on top of each. Take a small pinch of paprika with your fingers and sprinkle over each bowl.

SKILLS
♦ COUNTING
♦ SQUEEZING LEMONS
♦ WASHING VEGETABLES
♦ DIVIDING

pink fish sandwich

You can make these whenever you have some spare time in the day and then keep them in the fridge until you are ready to cook them. Instead of adding lemon zest to the breadcrumb mixture you could try lime, or to make green fish fingers add lots of fresh chopped herbs to the breadcrumbs. All three of my children insisted that this recipe went in the book, as they love making them with their friends!

For 4 people you need:

INGREDIENTS
8 thin salmon fillets (or white fish like haddock), cut into strips by an adult
2 free-range eggs
about 8 tablespoons breadcrumbs
1 unwaxed lemon or lime or handful fresh herbs
8 tablespoons plain/all-purpose flour
8 thick slices bread, some sliced tomatoes and watercress or lettuce

EQUIPMENT
scissors ◆ parchment paper
2 baking trays ◆ table knife
3 small bowls ◆ spoon ◆ fork
small grater ◆ oven mitts

1 Turn the oven on to 190°C (375°F) Gas 5. Cut 2 pieces of parchment paper, each big enough to cover the baking trays. Rub your finger all over the fish to check for bones. If you feel a sharp bone sticking out, pull it out with your fingers.

2 To crack open the eggs, hold an egg in one hand and carefully use a table knife to crack the egg in the middle. Put your thumbs into the crack and pull the egg shell apart. Let the egg fall into a small bowl. Repeat with the other egg. Fish out any egg shell with a spoon. Mix with a fork.

3 Put the breadcrumbs into a small bowl. To grate the lemon or lime, hold the handle of the grater with one hand and use the other hand to push the fruit downwards over the grater 'teeth'. Always keep your fingers away from the grater 'teeth', as they are very sharp. Add the zest to the breadcrumbs.

4 Count the spoons of flour into a small bowl. Dip all sides of the fish first into the flour, then the beaten egg, then the breadcrumbs so that the fish is well coated. Put the fish pieces on the baking trays.

4

Ask an adult to help you put the trays into the oven using oven mitts. Bake for 10–15 minutes or until the fish is golden and cooked all the way through – ask an adult to help you check this. Ask an adult to help you take the trays out of the oven using oven mitts. Put the fish pieces inside some bread with sliced tomatoes and watercress.

SKILLS
- BREADCRUMBING
- CRACKING EGGS
- USING OVEN
- ZESTING LEMON

STAGE
2

minty lamb couscous

This is great to make after you have had roast lamb for a Sunday dinner. However, if you haven't had a roast, you could try adding other ingredients instead like canned fish, crumbled feta cheese, chopped tomatoes, fresh herbs, chopped cucumber, watercress, grated carrot etc. and then mix with Susan's salad dressing from page 18 instead of the mint jelly.

For 4 people you need:

INGREDIENTS
200 g/1⅓ cups couscous
225 ml/1 cup boiling water (or just enough to cover the couscous)
2 large handfuls dried apricots
1 large courgette/zucchini or 2 small
about 3 teaspoons mint jelly
a few handfuls leftover roast lamb, chopped
freshly ground black pepper, if you like

EQUIPMENT
heatproof bowl • measuring jug/cups • fork • scissors grater

1 Weigh the couscous. How you weigh it will depend on the weighing scales that you use. (See pages 50 and 52 for more information about how to weigh ingredients.) Put the couscous into a heatproof bowl.

2 Ask an adult or older child to boil some water and pour the boiling water into a measuring jug/cup up to the 250-ml/1-cup mark. Pour this water carefully over the couscous. Leave the couscous for about 5 minutes and watch as the hard grains absorb the hot water and become soft and fluffy.

3 Use a fork or your hands to mix the couscous and break up the grains. The grains will feel lovely and soft!

4 Using scissors, snip the apricots into small pieces. To grate the courgette/zucchini, hold the handle of the grater with one hand and use the other hand to push the courgette downwards over the grater 'teeth'. Always keep your fingers away from the grater 'teeth', as they are very sharp. Add the courgettes and apricots to the couscous. Add the mint jelly and chopped roast lamb to the couscous and mix everything together. Taste the mixture and add a little black pepper if you think it needs it.

SKILLS ◆ PREPARING COUSCOUS ◆ MEASURING LIQUID USING SCISSORS ◆ GRATING

4

oven-baked herby burgers

Lots of children have helped to test the recipes in this book, especially Rosie, Libby and Tess. They all felt that the book should have a burger recipe in it and they found this oven-baked burger recipe easy to cook and good to eat.

1 Turn the oven on to 190°C (375°F) Gas 5. Dip a pastry brush into a little olive or vegetable oil and brush it all over a baking tray. This will stop the burgers from sticking to the tray.

2 Using a table knife, cut the cheese into small pieces on a cutting board.

3 Using scissors, snip the herbs into small pieces and put into a mixing bowl. Still using scissors, snip the ends off the spring onions/scallions and throw away, then snip the spring onions into tiny pieces and put in the bowl.

4 Now you need to crack open the egg: hold it in one hand and carefully use a table knife to crack the egg in the middle. Put your thumbs into the crack and pull the egg shell apart. Let the egg fall into a small bowl. Fish out any egg shell with a spoon. (See page 60 for a photo of how to crack eggs.) Mix with a fork.

5 Put the beef, chopped cheese and egg into the bowl with the herbs and spring onions/scallions and mix together really well with your hands.

6 Break the beef mixture in half and then break each piece in half again to make 4 pieces (quarters). Now break each quarter in half again to make 8 pieces (eighths). Roll each piece into a ball with your hands, then put onto the oiled baking tray and flatten into a burger shape. Do the same with all the

To make 8 small burgers you need:

INGREDIENTS

a little olive or vegetable oil
about 35 g/1 oz. Cheddar cheese
small handful fresh herbs e.g. parsley,
coriander/cilantro or thyme
2 spring onions/scallions
1 free-range egg
500 g/1 lb. good-quality mined/ground
beef (don't buy extra-lean otherwise
your burger will be too dry)
8 small burger buns, some lettuce, sliced
tomatoes and tomato ketchup

EQUIPMENT

pastry brush ◆ baking tray ◆ table knife
cutting board ◆ scissors ◆ mixing bowl
small bowl ◆ spoon ◆ fork ◆ palette knife
oven mitts

pieces. Now, WASH YOUR HANDS – you
must always wash your hands thoroughly
after handling raw meat. Ask an adult to
help you put the tray into the oven using
oven mitts. Cook for 8 minutes. Ask an adult
to help you take the tray out of the oven
using oven mitts. Using a palette knife, turn
the burgers over and put back in the oven
for 8 more minutes or until cooked in the
middle. Eat in buns with lettuce, tomatoes
and ketchup.

Tip: To make lamb burgers, swap the beef
for lamb and add thyme leaves, plus chopped
dried apricots instead of Cheddar cheese.

SKILLS

◆ CHOPPING WITH TABLE KNIFE
◆ USING SCISSORS
◆ CRACKING EGGS
◆ COUNTING
◆ DIVIDING
◆ SHAPING
◆ USING OVEN

STAGE
2

grilled/broiled ham bagel

Help your parents out by making your own snack or lunch. Just remember that the grill/broiler is hot and you must have an adult with you when you use it. Choose a favourite chutney to spread over the top. If your bagel is for lunch, try to have some chopped cucumber, celery or carrot with it. It is a good idea to have a vegetable or fruit with every meal and snack, so that you eat your '5 a day'.

To make 1 bagel you need:

INGREDIENTS
1 bagel, cut in half
1 slice ham
small piece Cheddar cheese
chutney, if you like

EQUIPMENT
baking tray • grater • oven mitts
table knife

SKILLS
◆ USING GRILL/BROILER
◆ GRATING
◆ SPREADING

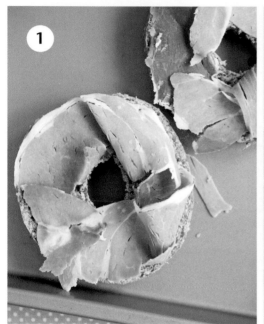

1 Turn the grill/broiler on — you will need to ask an adult to show you how to do this, as all grills/broilers are different. Put the bagel halves, cut-side up, onto a baking tray. Tear the ham and put onto the bagel halves around the holes in the middle. Avoid the hole otherwise the ham will fall into it!

2 To grate the cheese, hold the handle of the grater with one hand and use the other hand to push the cheese down over the grater 'teeth'. Keep your fingers away from the grater 'teeth', as they are very sharp. Sprinkle the cheese on the ham.

3 Ask an adult to help you put the baking tray under the grill/broiler using oven mitts. Grill/broil for 3–4 minutes or until the cheese is golden and bubbling. Keep watching it — this will only take a few minutes and if you leave it under the grill/broiler for too long it might burn. Ask an adult to help you take the tray from under the grill/broiler using oven mitts and see how the cheese has melted!

4 Spread a little chutney over the top.

tropical smoothie

Papayas have a green skin that turns yellow as it ripens and the orange flesh is sweet. Passion fruits are small and dark, and their skin wrinkles when it ripens. The skin can be quite tough, so you may need to ask for help with cutting through it. Most smoothies are made using a blender, but they have a very sharp blade that cuts the fruit into tiny pieces, so ask an adult to help you when you use one.

To make 2 glasses you need:

INGREDIENTS
1 ripe papaya (about 450 g/1 lb.)
1 passion fruit
1 ripe banana
2 small glasses fresh orange juice

EQUIPMENT
cutting board • small paring knife
spoon • blender • spoon • 2 tall glasses

SKILLS
◆ **USING BLENDER**
◆ **CHOPPING WITH PARING KNIFE**

1 Use the bridge-cutting technique to cut the papaya in half lengthwise: on a cutting board, make a 'bridge' with a thumb and finger of one hand and hold the papaya. Hold a small paring knife in your other hand and put the blade under the bridge, then cut downwards firmly. Cut the passion fruit in half in the same way. You might ask an adult or older child to help you, as passion fruits are quite tough. Using a spoon, scrape the black seeds out of the papaya and throw away.

2 Peel the banana, break it into 2 or 3 pieces and put into the blender. Using a teaspoon, scoop the orange papaya flesh into the blender, too. Now scrape the seeds and juice from the passion fruit on top of the papaya.

3 Pour the orange juice in the blender, put the lid on, and blend until smooth. (Ask an adult or older child to help you.)

4 Pour the smoothie into 2 tall glasses.

STAGE
2

Finley's lemonberryade

Finley likes to make this when we have friends over. The lemonade without the raspberries will keep for at least a week in a bottle in the fridge. If you do add raspberries, only add them when you are ready to drink the lemonade.

SKILLS
CHOPPING WITH PARING KNIFE
SQUEEZING LEMONS ◆ POURING
MEASURING LIQUIDS ◆ MASHING
USING SIEVE/STRAINER

1 You might like to ask an adult to help you with this, as lemons are quite tough to cut. Use the bridge-cutting technique to cut the lemons: on a cutting board, make a 'bridge' with a thumb and finger of one hand and hold the lemon. Hold a small paring knife in your other hand and put the blade under the bridge, then cut downwards firmly.

2 Put a lemon half over a lemon juicer and press down. Try to turn the lemon as you press down. If you don't have a lemon juicer, you might like to try cutting the lemon half in half again using the bridge-cutting technique to make quarters and then squeeze the lemon quarters with your hands.

3 Before you pour the juice into a jug/pitcher, if there are any seeds in the juice, pour it through a sieve/strainer into the jug/pitcher to catch the seeds.

4 Add the sugar to the jug/pitcher and stir with a big spoon until the sugar has dissolved (or disappeared).

5 Use a measuring jug/cup to measure 1 litre/4 cups cold water and add to the lemon juice in the jug/pitcher.

6 When you are ready to drink this, put the raspberries in a bowl and mash with a fork. Add them to the lemonade and stir. You need to strain the lemonade again into another jug/pitcher, pushing the raspberries though the sieve/strainer with a fork as you go.

5

6

To make 8 glasses you need:

INGREDIENTS

4 lemons
130 g/⅔ cup golden
caster/natural cane sugar
1 litre/4 cups cold water
handful fresh raspberries
ice cubes, if you want to make
the drink cold!

EQUIPMENT

cutting board ◆ small paring knife
lemon juicer ◆ small sieve/strainer
nice jug/pitcher ◆ big spoon ◆ fork
measuring jug/cups ◆ small bowl

Tips: If you are going to drink this lemonade as soon as you have made it, you could try using sparkling water to make it fizzy!

And now that you know how to juice fruit, you might like to make some freshly squeezed orange juice for breakfast.

STAGE
2

flower & herb ice bowl

I first made one of these in my home economics (now called design technology) lessons at school and I still remember how cool I thought it was to have made my own bowl. You could scoop your favourite ice cream or sorbet into the middle, or just put fresh summer fruits inside. Whatever you choose, I bet your friends will be impressed with the bowl. Remember, you will need to be patient and wait several hours until this is frozen.

To make 1 beautiful ice bowl you need:

INGREDIENTS
fresh edible flowers and/or fresh herbs or any pretty leaves from the garden (we used pink rose petals, rosemary, thyme and sage)
You might like to fill your bowl with a yogurt and fruit mix like the berry crunch on page 40, but you will need to make more to fill your ice bowl (without the cereal). You will also need lots of fresh raspberries and strawberries.

EQUIPMENT
big freezerproof bowl • small freezerproof bowl • small weight • sticky tape • clean kitchen towel • plate

1 Take your 2 bowls and pour enough cold water into the big bowl to half fill it. Scatter some fresh flowers and/or herbs in the water.
2 Rest the small bowl inside the big bowl and put a small weight in the small bowl to help it sit still. Stretch sticky tape across the tops of the bowls in several directions to hold the small bowl in place inside the big bowl. Put in the freezer and leave overnight.
3 The next day, peel off the sticky tape and carefully pull the small bowl out of the big bowl.
4 Lay a clean kitchen towel on the work surface and tip the big bowl upside down to let the ice bowl slip out. Turn the ice bowl the right way up and sit it on a plate. Fill your ice bowl with the yogurt and fruit mix and top with fresh raspberries and strawberries.

Tip: You might need to sit the big bowl in a little warm water to help ease the ice bowl out of it, but don't leave it sitting in warm water for long otherwise it will melt.

SKILLS
◆ FREEZING
◆ PICKING FRESH HERBS

fruit & seed bread

This is easy – you mix the wet ingredients together, then pour them into the dry ingredients. This is half like a cake and half like bread, but you don't need yeast like you do for bread. Look at page 88 for how to make pizza dough using yeast.

To make 2 small loaves you need:

INGREDIENTS
a little unsalted butter
300 ml/1¼ cups plain yogurt
2 free-range eggs
3 tablespoons sunflower oil
capful vanilla extract
100 g/⅔ cup dried fruit e.g. dried cranberries, raisins or chopped apricots or a mixture of all 3
150 g/1 cup chopped nuts, seeds or desiccated coconut or a mixture of all 3
250 g/2 cups self-raising/rising flour
125 g/½ cup plus 2 tablespoons golden caster sugar or granulated sugar
1 teaspoon baking powder

EQUIPMENT
parchment paper ◆ 2 x 500-g/1-lb. loaf tins/pans ◆ scissors ◆ table knife ◆ small bowl ◆ spoon ◆ fork ◆ measuring jug/cup mixing bowl ◆ wooden spoon ◆ oven mitts skewer

1 Turn the oven on to 180°C (350°F) Gas 4. Using a scrap of parchment paper, rub a little butter inside the loaf tins/pans. Using scissors, cut a piece of parchment paper to fit along the bottoms of the tins and up the ends. Fit it inside the tins – this will make it easy to pull the bread out after it's baked.
2 Spoon the yogurt into a measuring jug/cup and stop when the yogurt reaches the 300-ml/1¼-cup mark on the jug/cup.
3 Crack open the eggs: hold an egg in one hand and carefully use a table knife to crack the egg in the middle. Put your thumbs into the crack and pull the egg shell apart. Let the egg fall into a bowl. Repeat with the other egg. Fish out any egg shell with a spoon. (See page 60 for a photo of how to crack

5

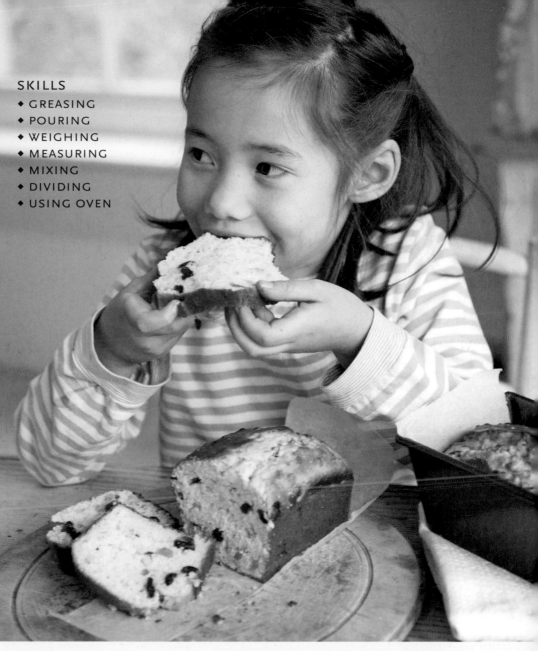

SKILLS
◆ GREASING
◆ POURING
◆ WEIGHING
◆ MEASURING
◆ MIXING
◆ DIVIDING
◆ USING OVEN

6

eggs.) Mix with a fork. Add the eggs, sunflower oil and vanilla to the yogurt and mix with a fork.

4 Weigh the dried fruit, nuts, flour and sugar. How you weigh them will depend on the weighing scales you use. (See pages 50 and 52 for more information about how to weigh ingredients.)

5 Put all the weighed dry ingredients – dried fruit, nuts, flour and sugar – into a mixing bowl. Add the baking powder and mix together. Pour the yogurt mixture into the mixing bowl, too.

6 Use the wooden spoon to mix everything together. Spoon half the mixture into one loaf tin/pan and the other half into the other tin. Ask an adult to help you put the loaf tins in the oven using oven mitts. Bake for about 30 minutes, or until golden and risen. Ask an adult to help you test if the breads are cooked by poking the middle with a skewer – it should come out clean. Let the breads cool down until they're cool enough to touch. Pull the ends of the parchment paper up at each end of the loaf tins and pull the bread out.

STAGE
2

shortbread shapes

If my children want to bake and we don't seem to have much in the cupboard, this is what they make. When you choose cutters, make sure they are about the same size, because if you put big shortbreads onto a baking tray with little shortbreads, the little ones will be cooked a long time before the big ones! This recipe makes a lot of shapes – the number will depend on the size of the cutters you use.

SKILLS ◆ CREAMING ◆ ROLLING ◆ CUTTING ◆ USING OVEN

To make lots of shortbread shapes you need:

INGREDIENTS
125 g/1 stick unsalted butter, soft
55 g/¼ cup golden caster sugar/natural cane sugar plus a little extra
capful vanilla extract
175 g/1⅓ cups plain/all-purpose flour
1 tablespoon milk

EQUIPMENT
scissors ◆ parchment paper baking tray ◆ mixing bowl wooden spoon ◆ rolling pin pound coin or 2 pennies shaped cutters ◆ fork oven mitts

1 Turn the oven on to 190°C (375°F) Gas 5. Cut a piece of parchment paper big enough to cover the baking tray.
2 Put the soft butter, sugar and vanilla extract in a mixing bowl and mix well with a wooden spoon until it becomes fluffy and paler in colour. This helps to beat air into the mixture.
3 Add the flour and milk to the bowl and mix until the mixture comes together to form a ball. You can do this with your hands or the wooden spoon.
4 Break the dough into 3 pieces. Sprinkle a little flour over the work surface and the rolling pin. Flatten one piece of dough with a rolling pin until it is the same thickness as a pound coin or 2 stacked pennies. Take the cutters you have chosen and, starting at the edge of the dough, push them down into the dough to cut out shapes. Repeat with the rest of the dough.
5 Carefully lift the shapes onto the baking tray, then press a fork gently onto the shortbread to make pretty patterns. Sprinkle a little sugar over the top of the shortbread. Ask an adult to help you put the sheet in the oven using oven mitts. Bake for 10 minutes (if they are small shapes) or 15 minutes (if they are big shapes), or until golden.

what's-in-season fruit crumble

One of the first things my mum taught me to make was a crumble. It's a great way to learn how to rub butter into flour. Once you know how to do this you can have a go at making pastry (see page 114). You can sprinkle this crumble mix on top of so many different fruits. Try to choose fruit that is in season – if you are not sure what that is, ask the person working in the produce section of your supermarket or go to a local farmers' market. Berries are easy to use as you don't need to chop them first.

1 Turn the oven on to 180°C (350°F) Gas 4. To make the fruit filling, use the bridge-cutting technique to cut the plums in half: on a cutting board, make a 'bridge' with a thumb and finger of one hand and hold the plum. Hold a small paring knife in your other hand and put the blade under the bridge, then cut downwards firmly. Move the plums around as you cut to avoid cutting through the stone. Take out the stones.
2 Put the plums into 2 small or 1 large ovenproof dish. Pour the orange juice over the plums, add the sugar and flour, and mix with a spoon or your hands.

3 To make the crumble topping, put the flour into a bowl, add the butter, and rub the butter into the flour with your fingers until it looks like fine breadcrumbs (see page 114 for photos showing you how to do this). This can take a few minutes. Add the oats, sugar and spice and mix with your fingers again.
4 Spoon the mixture over the top of the plums. Ask an adult to help you put the dishes into the oven using oven mitts. Bake for 25–30 minutes, or until the crumble topping is crisp, the plums are soft and the fruit juices are bubbling up around the edges.

4

SKILLS
- ◆ RUBBING IN
- ◆ CUTTING WITH KNIFE
- ◆ MIXING WITH SPOON
- ◆ SPRINKLING TOPPING

For 4–6 people you need:

FRUIT FILLING

seasonal fruit, e.g. 15 plums or about
600 g/1 lb. 4 oz. fresh or frozen berries
or about 12 peaches or nectarines

4 tablespoons orange juice

3 tablespoons light brown sugar

1 tablespoon plain/all-purpose flour

CRUMBLE TOPPING

150 g/1 cup plus 2 tablespoons plain/
all-purpose flour

100 g/6½ tablespoons unsalted butter,
chilled and cut into small pieces

2 handfuls oats (or muesli if you prefer)

4 tablespoons light brown sugar

1 teaspoon ground mixed spice/apple
pie spice or ground cinnamon

EQUIPMENT

cutting board ◆ small paring knife
spoon ◆ 2 small or 1 large ovenproof dish

STAGE
2

Ella's marshmallow & chocolate squares

Ella invented this recipe when she found marshmallows and chocolate in the cupboard. She asked me how much butter and syrup to add, then she did the rest! This is only to be eaten occasionally, as it is very sweet!

SKILLS ◆ MELTING CHOCOLATE ◆ MIXING ◆ SETTING IN FRIDGE

To make about 30 small pieces you need:

INGREDIENTS
12 digestive biscuits/graham crackers or ginger biscuits/cookies
50 g/¾ cup mini-marshmallows
150 g/1 cup dried fruit e.g. raisins, chopped mango, chopped apricots
100 g/3½ oz. milk chocolate
100 g/6½ oz. unsalted butter, chopped into big chunks
5 tablespoons golden/corn syrup

EQUIPMENT
mixing bowl ◆ large saucepan teaspoon ◆ wooden spoon parchment paper ◆ any cake tin/pan (round, square or loaf tin) ◆ scissors ◆ table knife

1

2

3

1 Using a scrap of parchment paper, rub a little butter inside the cake tin/pan. Now using scissors, cut a piece of parchment to fit along the bottom of the tin and up the ends. Fit it inside the tin. Put the digestive biscuits/graham crackers into a mixing bowl. Break them into small pieces. Add the mini-marshmallows and dried fruit.
2 Break the chocolate into small pieces and put into a large saucepan with the butter. Add the golden/corn syrup – you might need to use a teaspoon to scrape the syrup off the tablespoon.
3 Ask an adult to help you turn the hob/burner onto low heat and put the saucepan over it. Leave for a few minutes until the chocolate starts to melt. Stir with a wooden spoon until the mixture is smooth. Take the pan off the heat, add the fruit and stir everything together.
4 Spoon the mixture into the tin/pan and push it down with the spoon. Cover with parchment paper and put in the fridge for 4 hours or until hard – be patient while you wait for it to set. Pull the ends of the parchment paper up at each end of the tin and pull the mixture out – you may need to run a table knife along the sides to help release it from the tin. Cut into small pieces and put into a jar.

4

bumblebee cakes

Have you ever made butterfly cakes? My children and their friends have made a variation of the butterfly cake, the bumblebee. It's flavoured with orange, but you could just add vanilla if you prefer. Make them plain or with cocoa powder.

To make 10 bumblebee cakes you need:

CAKES
½ orange
125 g/1 stick unsalted butter, soft
125 g/1 generous cup golden caster sugar/natural cane sugar
capful vanilla extract
2 free-range eggs
125 g/1 cup self-raising/rising flour OR if you want to make them chocolatey use 100 g/¾ cup self-raising/rising flour and 25 g/¼ cup cocoa powder

BUTTERCREAM
½ orange
50 g/3 tablespoons unsalted butter, soft
125 g/1 scant cup icing/confectioners' sugar

TO DECORATE
chocolate buttons and chocolate matchsticks (or long thin sweets/candies)

EQUIPMENT
mixing bowl ◆ wooden spoon ◆ table knife
2 bowls ◆ large metal spoon ◆ 12-hole
cupcake tin/pan lined with 12 paper cases

1 Turn the oven on to 180°C (350°F) Gas 4. To make the cakes, squeeze the juice from the orange half into a mixing bowl and add the soft butter, sugar and vanilla extract. Mix well with a wooden spoon until it becomes fluffy and paler in colour. This helps to beat air into the mixture. Crack open the eggs: hold an egg in one hand and use a table knife to crack the egg in the middle. Put your thumbs into the crack and pull the egg shell apart. Let the egg fall into a bowl. Repeat with the other egg. Fish out any egg shell with a spoon. (See page 60 for a photo of how to crack eggs.)
2 Add the eggs to the butter mixture and beat. Add the flour and 'fold' in (see page 51) with a metal spoon.
3 Divide the batter evenly between the

cupcake cases with a spoon. Ask an adult to help you put the tin/pan in the oven using oven mitts. Bake for about 12–15 minutes until golden and slightly springy to the touch. Ask an adult to help you take the tin out of the oven using oven mitts and let cool.
4 Using a table knife, cut a small oval shape from the middle of each cake.

Cut this oval in half to make 2 wings.
5 To make the buttercream, squeeze the orange half into a bowl. Add the soft butter and sugar and mix well.
6 Spoon this into the holes in each cupcake, then stick the wings into the buttercream. Stick chocolate buttons and matchsticks into the cakes to make them look like bumblebees.

STAGE
2

Grown-ups: this page is for you

CHILDREN: YOU CAN SKIP THIS BIT AND HAVE FUN COOKING!

This age range is huge. Some children will be able to cook independently and others will still need some assistance. But here are a few things that your child will be beginning to do during this stage. Remind your child that she can go back to Stage 1 of the book as she will find those recipes easy to make.

• It is likely that your child will be well into the swing of following the recipes on her own by now, and will be gaining independence and confidence in the kitchen. This is what this book is all about!

• She will enjoy the chance to try new pieces of kitchen equipment. Try to stand back and let her feel that she is in control, at the same time being nearby if help is needed. It is very easy to take over in the kitchen, so try to hold back.

• By now, most children like to cook with a friend or sibling. The sooner children realize that cooking is a fun and sociable activity, the better!

• She will have an increased ability to remember and should be able to easily repeat skills from the previous chapters. These new skills will be with her now for life.

• Her coordination will be greatly improved and she will have more control over smaller muscles, making it easier to complete more intricate tasks.

• She will be able to plan ahead more easily, for example if she is helping to make a meal, she will have a better understanding of timing and planning.

• She is likely to be keen to understand more about the science behind food, for example about yeast and kneading, and about cake making.

• Children at this age still enjoy learning through play, which is just one reason why cooking is so great, as she can learn essential life skills while having fun in the kitchen.

• She will be able to start to teach other family members her new-found skills.

• Some children will be ready to cook a two- or even three-course meal for the family using the recipes from all the stages in this book – enjoy being cooked for!

• Make sure she helps to clear up after she has finished cooking! This is a really important life skill.

SKILLS

Here are more skills that you can learn and practise as you make the recipes in this chapter. You will also be using some skills from the previous chapters, but they will be so easy by now that you probably won't even realize you are using them.

PEELING VEGETABLES
Hold the fruit or vegetable in one hand and the peeler in the other hand. Press it onto the fruit or vegetable and push away from you. It is a good idea to practise peeling vegetables with different peelers to see which you find the easiest; there are lots of different kinds and some are easier to use than others.

KNEADING DOUGH
This means to bash and push the dough. This helps to move the yeast cells around the dough and makes it stretchy. You may need to knead for 10 minutes before the dough is ready. It should be smooth, stretchy and almost silky when you touch it. To test if the dough has been kneaded for long enough, roll it into a ball and prod it with your finger – it should spring back quickly.

MAKING A WHITE SAUCE
This is a great skill to learn, as once you know how to make a white sauce, you can then make a pasta meal for your family like the swirly pasta with leek, broccoli & cheese sauce on page 96. The best method is to make a 'roux', which is when you melt the butter in the pan, add the flour and then cook the flour and butter mixture to make a paste or 'roux'. You then add the milk to the paste and keep cooking. However, you can also try putting all the ingredients into the pan together. Use a balloon whisk to keep stirring the mixture over gentle heat until you have a smooth sauce. This is the 'all in one' method.

COOKING BASMATI RICE
This type of rice grows in India. You always want to use twice as much volume of water as rice. This means that if you want to cook 1 mug/cup of rice, you will need 2 mugs/cups of water. Put the rice and water into a saucepan and cover with the lid. Bring to a boil and then lower the heat under the pan until the rice is simmering. Cook for 14 minutes, then very carefully take the pan off the heat and stand it on a heatproof pan stand/trivet for 10 minutes. You should have white, fluffy rice at the end.

ROLLING UP SUSHI
This is great fun and gets easier the more you practice. Gently roll the seaweed around the rice and filling and gently press together.

LADLING
Sometimes it is easiest to use a ladle to transfer food like stew or soup from one container to another. A ladle is like a small bowl with a handle.

BASHING GARLIC
If you don't have a garlic press or if you prefer to keep the garlic clove whole – like for the lemony chicken recipe on page 110 – you can always just squash the garlic slightly to release some of its juices and flavour and keep it whole. Bash the clove of garlic with the end of a rolling pin to loosen the papery skin. Peel off the skin and throw away. Now bash the clove again with the end of the rolling pin to split the garlic slightly. Remember to wash the rolling pin.

BAKING POTATOES
Always prick the potatoes with a fork first and bake them in a very hot oven so that the skins are crisp and the insides are soft and fluffy.

SEPARATING EGGS
This is when you want to separate the yolks and the whites in the eggs. There are different ways to do this. For example, take 2 bowls. Crack the egg over one bowl and then carefully tip the white and yolk from one shell half into the other. As you move the egg between the shells, let the white gradually drop into the bowl until you're just left with the yolk in the egg shell. Now drop the yolk into the second bowl. Alternatively, you may prefer to crack the egg onto a saucer and then cover the yolk with a small bowl. Tip the saucer so that the white drips into a bowl, leaving the yolk behind on the saucer.

ROASTING
To roast something in the oven means to cook it at a high temperature with only a little fat, like olive oil.

you cook it. The marinade will help to keep the meat or fish juicy as it cooks.

WHISKING EGG WHITES
If you are using a balloon whisk to whisk egg whites, you might need to pass the whisk to a friend and take it in turns to stop your wrist from aching. If you use an electric mixer, it is much quicker!

WHY DO CAKES RISE?
When you beat together the butter and sugar and then beat in the eggs, you are adding air to the batter. When you bake the cake, the air inside the bubbles gets bigger, helping the cake to rise. Many cakes use self-raising/rising flour and sometimes baking powder too. These both contain carbon dioxide, which is released as a gas when it is heated. As the carbon dioxide becomes a gas, it gets bigger and pushes the cake up, making it rise.

MELTING CHOCOLATE
Find a small bowl that will sit on top of a saucepan so that the bottom of the bowl is just under the rim of the pan. Break the chocolate into small pieces (this helps it to melt quickly and evenly) and put into the small bowl. Half fill the saucepan with water, put the bowl of chocolate on top and bring it to a gentle simmer. Leave for a few minutes, then turn the heat off. Stir the chocolate carefully until it has melted. If the chocolate gets too hot, the cocoa butter will begin to separate from the cocoa solids, and the chocolate can become dry and crumbly. It is really important that you do not let any liquid like water drip into the chocolate – even a tiny amount can cause the chocolate to harden and turn into a solid lump! If this happens you will need to start again.

SETTING A TABLE FOR A MEAL
If you are serving a starter and a main course, you will need to lay two sets of cutlery at the table. Put the knife and fork on the table as normal and then lay a smaller knife and fork on the outside of this cutlery for the appetizer. When you eat a meal with more than one course, start with the cutlery on the outside and work your way into the middle.

COOKING PASTA
You will need the biggest pan that you can find so that the pasta has plenty of room to move around in the water as it cooks. This will help to make sure that it cooks evenly. See page 94 for more information about how to cook pasta.

DRAINING
You will need an adult or older child to help you drain pasta, as the saucepan will be heavy and the water will be very hot. Try to wear oven mitts to help prevent the water from splashing on your hands. Rest the colander in the sink and then very carefully pour the pasta and hot water into the colander.

MARINATING
A marinade can be made from a variety of ingredients, but it often contains an acid like lemon juice and an oil, plus a few other ingredients to add flavour. Add the meat or fish and leave to marinate for a little while to make sure that the flavours soak into the food before

KITCHEN EQUIPMENT

You have already used most of the basic kitchen utensils, but there are just a few other utensils that are worth mentioning in case you choose to cook all the recipes in this chapter.

PAN STAND/TRIVET
As it sounds, this is a small heatproof stand for resting hot pans on. It is very handy to have a pan stand/trivet by the hob/stovetop. You can then take something out of the oven and put it on the stand/trivet. Never put anything hot onto the kitchen work surface, as you might damage the surface.

PASTA PAN
A pasta pan has its own colander inside the pan, ready for draining the pasta when it is cooked. Most Italians have a pasta pan, as they like to cook pasta a lot. It doesn't matter if you don't have one – just use a large pan and a colander instead. (Always ask an adult to drain the pasta for you, as the pan will be heavy and full of boiling water.)

ROASTING DISH
Ideally you need a heavy-based roasting dish. This will heat up and cook the food without burning it.

WOK OR FRYING PAN/SKILLET
Now that you are used to cooking on the hob/stovetop, you might like to try making the stir-fry on page 92. The best pan for a stir-fry is a wok, as it is large enough to give you space to toss the vegetables around and 'stir' them as you 'fry'. If you don't have a wok, you could use a large frying pan/skillet.

FLUTED CUTTERS
Some cook stores sell these individually, or you could buy a set so that you have different-sized cutters to play with.

12-HOLE CUPCAKE TIN/PAN
This tin is ideal for making small cakes or tarts. Once you know how to make pastry, you can make up your own tart recipe.

2 x 20-CM/8-INCH CAKE TINS/PANS
If you only have one cake tin/pan and you want to make a layer cake like a Victoria sponge where you sandwich 2 cakes together, you need to make half the batter and bake it, then make the other half and bake it. Or you can see if a neighbour or friend has another cake tin you could use.

SUSHI MAT OR NAPKIN
If you don't have to have a sushi mat, you can use a napkin instead. A sushi mat is used to roll the sushi into a long sausage shape.

BOWLS FOR MARINATING
When you marinate fish, meat or vegetables, put the marinade ingredients in a glass, Pyrex, melamine or plastic bowl, not a metal one. Acidic ingredients like lemon juice and vinegar can react with the metal and give the food a funny taste.

WHISKS
You will need either a balloon whisk or an electric mixer to whisk egg whites until they are white and fluffy. I always recommend that if possible you have a go at whisking with a balloon whisk to practise how to whisk. You can always use an electric mixer later to see the difference.

SMALL PUDDING BASINS
These are good to have for making small baked desserts or you could use them for setting jellies. You might also hear an adult suggest that you use ramekins. These are small dishes that can be put into the oven.

VEGETABLE PEELER
These can be quite tricky to use, so you may need to have a go with friends' peelers until you find one that you are happy with.

SMALL GRATER
Some big graters have small holes on them that you can use for grating ingredients that you want to make tiny pieces from. If your big grater doesn't have small enough holes, you will need a small grater.

ham & pineapple pizzas

We often have these on a Saturday night. They are fun to make and cheaper than going out for pizza in a restaurant. Did you know that yeast is alive? It is a living micro-organism used to make bread rise and give it a lighter, more open texture. For the yeast to work, it needs to grow (or reproduce). To do this it needs warmth (from warm water), moisture (water) and food (sugar from the flour). The yeast produces a gas, carbon dioxide, which makes the bread rise before it is baked. We bake pizzas in a very hot oven to kill the yeast so that they don't carry on rising.

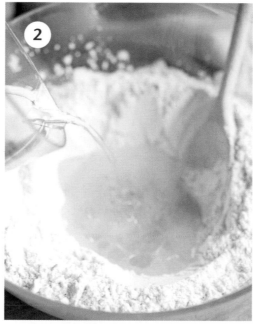

1 Put the flour into a mixing bowl. Sprinkle the yeast over the top.

2 Make a well (a hole) in the middle of the flour with your hand. Pour the warm water into a measuring jug/cup until it just reaches the 200-ml/1-cup mark. Make sure the water is warm and not too hot – when you put your finger in, it should feel just warm. Add the olive oil to the water, then pour into the well. Use a wooden spoon to stir the liquid and the flour will gradually fall into the water. Keep stirring until all the flour is mixed with the liquid and you have a dough.

3 Sprinkle a little flour over the work surface, take the dough out of the bowl and knead it. The best way to knead is to push the dough down and away with the heel of the hand and then pull it back with your fingers. Push it back onto the work surface, turn the dough slightly and then repeat. After a few minutes of doing this, the dough should have a smooth, elastic texture.

4 Clean the mixing bowl and put the dough back in. Cover it with clingfilm/plastic wrap or a clean kitchen towel and leave it somewhere warm to rise for about an hour, or until it is twice as big – look how much the dough has grown in the picture!

5 Turn the oven on to 200°C (400°F) Gas 6. Dip a pastry brush into a little olive oil and brush it all over the baking trays. Break the risen dough in half and, using a rolling pin, roll each piece into two large flat circles.

6 Lift the pizza crusts onto the baking trays. Spread the tomato passata/purée over the crusts with the back of a spoon.

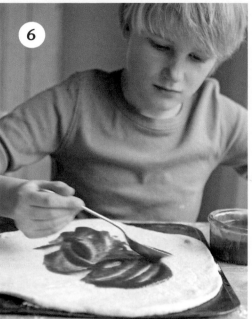

7 Scatter your ham and pineapple over the tomato passata/purée. Using oven mitts, put the trays in the oven and bake for 15–20 minutes or until the crusts are cooked.

To make 2 very large or 3–4 small pizzas you need:

PIZZA DOUGH
350 g/2¾ cups strong plain white flour/all-purpose flour

7-g packet/1¼ teaspoons 'easy bake'/ instant yeast

2 tablespoons olive oil plus a little extra

200 ml/1 scant cup warm (not hot) water

TOPPINGS
tomato passata/purée, ham, pineapple, mozzarella and grated cheese OR tomato passata/purée, prawns/shrimp and sliced (bell) peppers OR any other topping combinations that you might like to try

EQUIPMENT
mixing bowl • measuring jug/cup wooden spoon • clingfilm/plastic wrap pastry brush • 2 baking trays • rolling pin • spoon • oven mitts

Did you know? Kneading the dough helps to distribute the yeast cells evenly and give the dough elasticity (which means it is stretchy). You may need to knead for up to 10 minutes before the dough is smooth, elastic and almost silky to touch. To test if the dough has been kneaded for long enough, roll it into a ball and prod it with your finger – it should spring back quickly.

SKILLS
◆ MAKING YEAST DOUGH
◆ ROLLING
◆ SPREADING
◆ USING OVEN

STAGE
3

tacos with soya beans

The mild chilli powder in this recipe gives the beans a slight chilli flavour, but you can always leave it out if you really don't like it – they will still taste good. This simple meal is as fun to make as it is to eat because there are lots of things to assemble, and so lots of things to try!

For 4 people you need:

INGREDIENTS
400 g/14 oz. canned chopped
tomatoes
2 x 400-g/14-oz. cans soya/soybeans
in water (or cannellini/pinto beans)
2 spring onions/scallions
1 garlic clove
1 tablespoon olive oil
1 teaspoon ground coriander
1 teaspoon mild chilli powder
1 teaspoon sugar
handful coriander/cilantro leaves plus
a little extra
8–12 tacos
2 ripe avocados
150 ml/⅔ cup sour cream
grated Cheddar cheese
pieces of lime

EQUIPMENT
*can opener • colander • small paring
knife • cutting board • garlic press
small saucepan • wooden spoon
baking tray • oven mitts • spoon*

SKILLS
OPENING CANS • CUTTING
CRUSHING GARLIC • USING
HOB/STOVETOP AND OVEN

1 Turn the oven on to 180°C (350°F)
Gas 4. Use a can opener to open the
cans of tomatoes and beans. The
first time you do this you will need
an adult to show you how to use
your can opener, as they are all
slightly different. Drain the beans
in a colander.
2 Using the claw-cutting technique
(see page 50), cut the ends off the
spring onions/scallions with a small
paring knife and throw away. Cut the
spring onions into thin slices.

3 Peel the garlic clove and crush it
with a garlic press.
4 Put the oil and spring onions/
scallions into a small pan over low
heat on the hob/stovetop. Heat gently
for about 5 minutes, stirring every
now and then with a wooden spoon,
until they are soft. Add the crushed
garlic, ground coriander and chilli
powder and cook for another minute.
5 Add the tomatoes, drained beans,
sugar and coriander/cilantro leaves.
Turn the heat up. When the tomatoes

are bubbling, lower the heat and let
simmer gently for 10 minutes.
6 Put the tacos on a baking tray and,
using oven mitts, put them in the
oven for 3 minutes to heat up. Scoop
the stones out of the avocados with
a teaspoon and peel away the skins.
Using the claw-cutting technique,
cut the avocados into slices. Put the
beans, sour cream, cheese, extra
coriander/cilantro, avocado and lime
in bowls. Let everyone make their
own tacos.

STAGE
3

rainbow stir-fry

I have used ready-prepared vegetables here so all you need to prepare are the leeks and green beans. When you have practised using a small sharp knife, you may like to add other vegetables like sliced red or yellow (bell) peppers or bok choy.

For 4 people you need:

INGREDIENTS

1 leek, trimmed and washed
about 200 g/1½ cups green beans
2 large handfuls coriander/cilantro leaves
2 garlic cloves
small piece ginger, about 2.5 cm/1 inch
2 teaspoons sesame oil
2 teaspoons olive oil
about 300 g/10 oz. crunchy vegetable stir-fry mix (package sizes will vary; the amount doesn't have to be exact)
300 g/10 oz. pre-cooked free-range egg noodles
2 large handfuls pine nuts or peanuts, if you like
1–2 tablespoons low-salt soy sauce

EQUIPMENT

*small paring knife • cutting board
scissors • garlic press • small grater
wok or large frying pan/skillet • wooden spoon*

1 Use the bridge-cutting technique to cut the leeks in half widthwise, then lengthwise with a small paring knife. Using the claw-cutting technique, thinly slice the leeks.

2 Using scissors, snip the coriander/cilantro into small pieces. Still using scissors, cut the ends off the beans and throw them away. Cut the beans in half.

3 Peel the garlic clove and crush it with a garlic press. Grate the ginger using a small grater (you don't need to peel it first).

4 Turn the hob/burner to medium heat. Heat the oils in a wok or large frying pan/skillet. Add the leeks and fry for a few minutes, stirring with a wooden spoon. Add the garlic, ginger and beans and fry for another minute.

5 Add the vegetable stir-fry mix and fry for another minute. Add the noodles, coriander/cilantro, nuts and soy sauce and fry for a few minutes, stirring as you fry.

SKILLS
- KNIFE SKILLS
- STIR-FRYING
- GRATING
- CRUSHING GARLIC
- PREPARING VEGETABLES

how to cook pasta

Knowing how to cook pasta is a great skill, as it is so easy to make it into a lovely meal. However, you will need help from an adult, as the pasta pan will be very heavy and full of hot water!

For 1 person you need:
INGREDIENTS
75–115 g/2½–4 oz. dried pasta

EQUIPMENT
the biggest saucepan you have • jug/pitcher • long-handled or wooden spoon

a Ideally you need 1 litre/4 cups of water for every 100 g/3½ oz. pasta, but this will only work if you have a pan big enough for this amount of water. However, only ever fill your saucepan three-quarters full. Don't fill it to the top or it will overflow when you add the pasta!

b Find the biggest saucepan that you have in your kitchen (the pasta needs to be cooked in a large pan to help make sure that it cooks evenly; if the pan is too small, some of the pasta may be trapped at the bottom of the pan and it will cook more quickly than the pasta at the top). Turn the hob/burner to medium heat and put the pan of water on it. Heat the water until it comes to a boil – you will know that it is boiling when you can see the water bubbling.

c Put your pasta into a jug/pitcher and then carefully add the pasta to the water (keep your hands away from the hot water!). Using a long-handled spoon, gently swirl the pasta around in the pan to help stop it from sticking together. Bring the water back to a boil and cook following the packet instructions (all pastas have different cooking times). Use a fork to take a piece of pasta from the pan, let cool slightly and then test to see if it is ready: when you bite into it, it should be cooked but still have a little 'bite' – this is known as 'al dente' in Italy. When it is cooked, put a colander in the sink and ask an adult to pour the pasta into the colander for you (remember, the pan will be very heavy) to drain it.

pasta sauces

pepper pasta sauce

You need to use just plain roasted (bell) peppers for this recipe, not antipasti peppers that have lots of oils and herbs added to them.

For 4 people you need:
INGREDIENTS
10 oz. roasted red (bell) peppers from a jar
300 g/10 oz. pasta shapes, cooked and drained (see opposite for instructions)
handful fresh basil or coriander/cilantro leaves
handful baby spinach leaves
4 tablespoons cream cheese

EQUIPMENT
colander • scissors • saucepan wooden spoon

Drain the roasted peppers in a colander in the sink. Using scissors, snip the peppers into really small pieces (the smaller the better) and add to the cooked and drained pasta in the saucepan. Tear the basil or coriander/cilantro leaves and spinach into small pieces and add to the pasta with the cream cheese. Put the pan over low heat and cook until the cream cheese has melted, stirring gently with a wooden spoon.

tuna pasta sauce

This is one of my daughter Lola's favourite quick suppers, and she also loves it cold in her packed lunchbox for school.

For 4 people you need:
INGREDIENTS
150 g/1 cup canned or frozen (and defrosted) sweetcorn/corn kernels
2 x 185-g/6-oz. cans tuna, drained
3–4 tablespoons mayonnaise
300 g/10 oz. pasta shapes, cooked and drained (see opposite for instructions)

EQUIPMENT
can opener • colander • bowl fork • spoon

Use a can opener to open the can of sweetcorn/corn kernels. The first time you do this you will need an adult to show you how to use your can opener, as they all differ slightly. If you are using frozen corn, you will need to let it defrost for at least 1 hour before you make the pasta sauce. Use the can opener to open the cans of tuna. Drain both the corn and tuna in a colander, then tip into a bowl. Break the tuna up with a fork, add the mayonnaise and mix. Spoon the mixture over the cooked pasta and mix well.

STAGE
3

swirly pasta with leek, broccoli & cheese sauce

It's useful to know how to make a white sauce like this one because it is used in many dishes like lasagne, mac and cheese, cauliflower cheese etc.

1 Turn the oven on to 190°C (375°F) Gas 5. Use the claw-cutting technique to cut the broccoli into chunks with a small paring knife. Using the same technique, slice the leek into thin slices.
2 Turn the hob/burner onto a low heat. Put the leek and butter into a saucepan and heat gently. Cook for about 10 minutes, or until the leek has softened. Stir with a wooden spoon. Add the flour.
3 Stir and cook for a few minutes until you have a thick paste. Now take a balloon whisk and, whisking all the time, slowly pour in the milk. Keep whisking until you have a smooth sauce and cook gently for a few minutes. Add the mustard and almost all the cheese (keep some for the top) to the sauce, stir and take off the heat.
4 Cook the pasta following the instructions on page 94. Add the broccoli to the pasta pan 2 minutes before the pasta has finished cooking. When it is cooked, put a colander in the sink and ask an adult to pour the pasta and broccoli into the colander for you. Tip the pasta and broccoli from the colander into an ovenproof dish. Pour the sauce over the top and sprinkle the last bit of cheese over it. Using oven mitts, put the dish in the oven. Cook for 25–30 minutes until the topping is golden and the sauce is bubbling.

For 4 people you need:

INGREDIENTS

300 g/10 oz. tender stem
broccoli/broccolini

1 leek, trimmed and washed

50 g/3 tablespoons unsalted butter

50 g/⅓ cup plain/all-purpose flour

500 ml/2 cups whole milk

1 teaspoon English mustard

2 large handfuls grated Cheddar or
hard cheese

250 g/8 oz. pasta spirals

EQUIPMENT

*small paring knife • cutting board
saucepan • wooden spoon • balloon whisk
colander • ovenproof dish • oven mitts*

SKILLS

◆ CHOPPING
◆ MAKING WHITE SAUCE
◆ COOKING PASTA
◆ USING OVEN

STAGE
3

easy minestrone soup

The great thing about this soup is that you don't have to blend it at the end of cooking. It's ready to eat just as it is, all lovely and chunky.

For 4 people you need:

INGREDIENTS
4 spring onions/scallions
1 garlic clove
1 tablespoon olive oil
500g/2 cups passata/tomato purée
1 teaspoon sugar
390-g/14-oz. can soya/soybeans in water
100 g/¾ cup small pasta for soup
2 large handfuls frozen peas
2 tablespoons pesto
handful grated Parmesan

EQUIPMENT
*small paring knife • cutting board
rolling pin • garlic press • heavy-based
saucepan • wooden spoon*

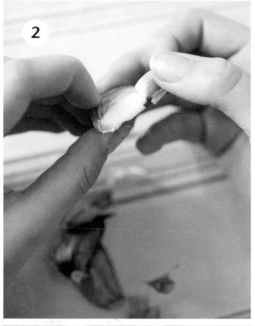

1 Using the claw-cutting technique, cut the ends off the spring onions/scallions with a small paring knife and throw away. Now slice the spring onions/scallions into thin slices.
2 Bash the garlic clove with a rolling pin, then peel off the skin.
3 Crush the garlic using a garlic press.
4 Turn the hob/burner to low heat. Heat the oil in a heavy-based saucepan. Fry the spring onions/scallions and garlic for 2 minutes, stirring occasionally with a wooden spoon. Pour the passata/tomato purée into the pan. Fill the tomato container with water and pour into the pan. Do this twice. Add the sugar.
5 Add the beans. Turn the heat up to high and cook until the mixture is simmering. Lower the heat and simmer gently for 15 minutes.
6 Add the pasta, peas and pesto and cook for another 5 minutes (or however long the pasta packet says). Sprinkle the grated Parmesan on top.

Tip: To add green beans instead of peas, cut the ends off using scissors, then cut the beans into small pieces before you put them into the soup.

5

6

SKILLS
- ◆ CUTTING
- ◆ USING STOVETOP
- ◆ CRUSHING GARLIC
- ◆ USING SCISSORS

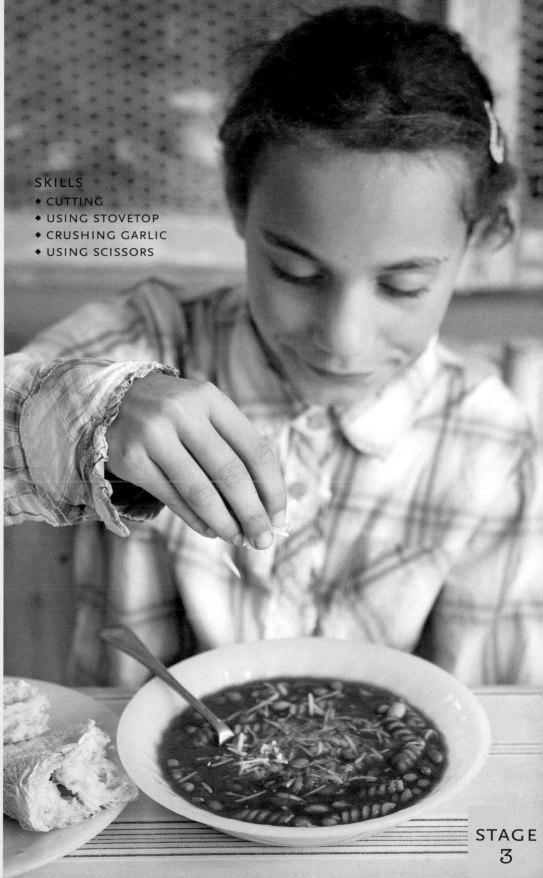

STAGE
3

fish curry with rice

Have you ever been to a curry house? You may think that all curries are hot and spicy, but they are not. They can be mild and creamy and taste delicious like this.

For 4 people you need:

INGREDIENTS
big handful coriander/cilantro leaves
3 spring onions/scallions
1 tablespoon olive oil
3 tablespoons mild curry paste
400 g/14 oz. canned chopped tomatoes
200 ml/1 scant cup hot vegetable stock or hot water
large handful few different vegetables e.g. baby corn and green beans
300 g/10 oz. mixed fresh fish fillets e.g. haddock, salmon, monkfish, cut into big chunks, or raw peeled prawns/shrimp
cooked long-grain rice (see opposite for instructions)
naan bread, poppadoms and mango chutney, to serve

EQUIPMENT
scissors ◆ small paring knife ◆ cutting board ◆ large saucepan ◆ wooden spoon

1 Using scissors, snip the coriander/cilantro into small pieces. Using the bridge-cutting technique, slice the vegetables in half lengthwise with a small paring knife. Using the claw-cutting technique, cut the ends off the spring onions/scallions. Cut the spring onions into thin slices. Turn the hob/burner to low heat. Put the spring onions and oil in a large saucepan on the hob/stovetop and heat gently.
2 Add the curry paste and fry for a few minutes, stirring with a wooden spoon.
3 Add the canned tomatoes to the pan, then fill the can with the hot stock or water and add to the pan, too. Simmer for 10 minutes, stirring once or twice.
4 Add the vegetables and cook for 5 minutes. Add the fish and cook until it is cooked – this will only be 5 minutes as you don't want to overcook it. Ask an adult to help you check if it is cooked. Add the coriander/cilantro and stir. Serve with rice, naan, poppadoms and chutney.

how to cook rice

For 2 people you need:

INGREDIENTS
1 tall glass of long-grain rice

EQUIPMENT
tall glass ◆ saucepan

a Measure 1 tall glass or cup of rice. Put the rice and then 2 glasses of water into a saucepan. Turn the hob/burner to medium heat and put the pan on the hob/stovetop.

b Bring the water in the pan up to a boil, lower the heat, put the lid on the pan and simmer for 14 minutes. Ask an adult to help you take the pan off the hob/stovetop and leave for 10 minutes with the lid on. The rice will continue to steam and become fluffy. Don't take the lid off during this time – it is important that the lid stays on if you want fluffy rice.

STAGE
3

super sushi rolls

This looks so impressive and yet it is easy and great fun to make. You will need to look for the ingredients in a good supermarket. Read the cooking instructions on the packet of sushi rice before you cook it, but my method below is how most sushi rice is cooked so it's likely to be similar.

1 To cook the rice, put the water and rice into a large saucepan over medium heat on the hob/stovetop. Heat until the water comes to a boil – you will know it is boiling when the water is bubbling. Cover the pan with the lid, lower the heat and simmer for 10 minutes. Take the pan off the hob/stovetop and let stand for 15 minutes with the lid on. Spoon the rice into a mixing bowl. In a small bowl, mix together the vinegar, sugar and salt. Pour the vinegar dressing over the rice, mix together and let cool.

2 Put a sheet of nori seaweed on a sushi mat. Use your hands or a spoon to cover two-thirds of the seaweed with rice. Leave a strip along the end of the seaweed furthest from you without rice. Press the rice down so that it is quite flat and evenly spread out.

3 Put a few strips of avocado and some prawns/shrimp along the middle.

4 Pick up the edge of the mat closest to you and roll up the seaweed and its filling into a big sausage. Use the mat to help you roll the seaweed neatly.

5 Squash the roll to make the sushi nice and compact, then unroll the mat. Do all this again with the remaining sheets of seaweed, rice and filling. Using the claw-cutting technique, cut each roll of sushi into 5 or 6 pieces with a small paring knife and serve with pickled ginger and soy sauce, if you like.

SKILLS

COOKING SUSHI RICE
ROLLING UP SUSHI ◆ CUTTING

To make about 30 pieces you need:

RICE

450 ml/2 cups water
225 g/1 generous cup Japanese rice for sushi
2 tablespoons rice wine vinegar
1 tablespoon golden caster/natural cane sugar
pinch salt
6 sheets nori seaweed

FILLINGS

ripe avocado strips and small, cooked prawns/
shrimp OR smoked salmon and thin
cucumber strips OR try thin strips of omelette
You might like to eat your sushi with pickled
ginger and soy sauce

EQUIPMENT

large saucepan ◆ timer ◆ spoon ◆ mixing bowl
small bowl ◆ spoon ◆ sushi mat ◆ small paring
knife

STAGE
3

Great granny's smoked haddock & spinach potato skins

Have you ever baked a potato before? A good baked potato should have a crisp skin and a light, fluffy middle. To achieve this you will need to bake them for an hour in a hot oven. My granny taught me to make these when I was little. It was the first time I had ever cooked fish and I still remember how good it felt.

For 4 people you need:

INGREDIENTS
4 baking potatoes
3 smoked haddock fillets
a little unsalted butter
2 large handfuls baby spinach leaves
handful fresh herbs e.g. parsley or fennel tops
½ lemon
3 tablespoons sour cream or crème fraîche
or a little butter

EQUIPMENT
fork • ovenproof dish • spoons • oven mitts
timer • scissors • mixing bowl • lemon juicer
table knife • clean napkin • roasting dish

1 Turn the oven on to 190°C (375°F) Gas 5. Prick the potatoes all over with a fork.
2 Put the smoked haddock into an ovenproof dish and dot with a little butter using teaspoons.
3 Using oven mitts, put the potatoes as well as the haddock into the oven. Set a timer for 15 minutes. Using oven mitts, take the haddock out of the oven and put to one side. Set the timer for 45 minutes more for the potatoes.
4 Using scissors, snip the herbs into small pieces and put into a mixing bowl. Tear the spinach into small pieces and put to one side. Squeeze the lemon half over a lemon juicer and pour the juice over the herbs. Add the sour cream. When the fish is cool enough to handle, peel the flesh away from the skin and flake the fish into

the bowl. Mix everything together with a fork.

5 Using oven mitts, take the potatoes out of the oven. Let cool slightly. Holding a potato with a clean napkin or oven mitt, use a table knife to cut the potato in half. Use a spoon to scoop the middle of the potato out of the potato skin and into the bowl with the haddock and herbs. Squash the chopped spinach into the potato skins. Mix the haddock mixture and cooked potato together in the bowl. Now spoon it back into the potato skins on top of the spinach. You will need to spoon the mixture between the potato skins. Using oven mitts, put the dish back in the oven and set the timer for another 10 minutes. Using oven mitts, take them out of the oven.

SKILLS

- ◆ USING SCISSORS
- ◆ BAKING POTATOES
- ◆ COOKING FISH
- ◆ SQUEEZING LEMONS
- ◆ USING OVEN
- ◆ SHARING

STAGE
3

beef & corn tortilla tubes

These are lots of fun to make and eat! The corn tortillas become all lovely and crisp when you bake them in the oven. (You will need to use corn tortillas, not flour ones.) This is delicious with the green dip on page 30.

To make 8 tubes you need:

INGREDIENTS
1 red onion
1 garlic clove
3 carrots, well washed
1 tablespoon olive oil plus a little extra
500 g/1 lb. minced/ground beef
500 g/2 cups passata/tomato purée
pinch brown sugar
8 corn tortillas
salad and Green Dip (page 30), to serve

EQUIPMENT
small paring knife • cutting board • garlic press grater • frying pan/skillet • wooden spoon ovenproof dish • oven mitts

1 Turn the oven on to 190°C (375°F) Gas 5. Peel the onion. Use the bridge-cutting technique to halve it with a paring knife. Using the claw-cutting technique, thinly slice it. Peel the garlic and crush it with a garlic press. Grate the carrots.

2 Put the oil, onion, garlic and carrots into a heavy-based frying pan/skillet over low heat on the hob/stovetop. Heat until soft.

3 Add the beef and fry for 10 minutes, or until it's turning golden brown. Add the passata/tomato purée and sugar, cover the pan with a lid, and cook gently for 10 minutes. The mixture will be quite dry, which is what you want.

4 Lay the tortillas on the cutting board and spoon some beef along the middle. Roll the tortillas around the beef and put into an ovenproof dish. Brush the tortilla tubes with a little oil. Using oven mitts, put the dish into the oven and cook for 15 minutes.

SKILLS • CUTTING • CRUSHING GARLIC • FRYING • ROLLING USING OVEN

all-in-one chicken

My girls really enjoy making a meal for the whole family to eat together, but they don't want to always spend long making it. This is why we came up with this recipe idea. To keep it really simple, put some baking potatoes into the oven to cook alongside the chicken. This is also delicious with couscous (see page 62), rice (see page 101) or salad (see page 18).

For 4 people you need:

INGREDIENTS
185 g/1 cup pitted black olives
300 g/10 oz. roasted red (bell) peppers from a jar
2 sprigs fresh rosemary
2 tablespoons olive oil
400 g/14 oz. canned chopped tomatoes
2 garlic cloves
4 free-range chicken pieces e.g. thighs or legs
baked potatoes, rice or mashed potatoes, or bread and salad, to serve

EQUIPMENT
colander ◆ scissors
mixing bowl ◆ garlic press
roasting dish ◆ oven mitts

1 Turn the oven on to 180°C (350°F) Gas 4. Tip the olives (if they need draining) and roasted peppers into a colander over a mixing bowl to drain. Now pour the liquid out of the bowl.
2 Using scissors, snip the peppers into small pieces and put into the dry mixing bowl.
3 Add the rosemary, olive oil and tomatoes to the peppers, then squash the olives slightly to break them up and add to the bowl, too. Peel the garlic cloves and crush them with a garlic press. Add the crushed garlic to the bowl.

4 Using your fingers, pull the skin off the chicken, throw the skin away, then add the chicken to the bowl.
5 Mix everything with your hands to coat the chicken in the pepper and olive mixture. Now WASH YOUR HANDS. Tip everything into a roasting dish. Using oven mitts, put the dish in the oven and cook for 35–45 minutes (depending on the size of the chicken pieces), or until the chicken is cooked all the way through – ask an adult to help you check this.

STAGE
3

lemony chicken

To make a marinade, you normally mix together an acid, like lemon juice or vinegar with an oil, like olive oil, sunflower oil or sesame oil. You then add some flavour with chopped herbs, spices or garlic. The marinade helps to keep the food juicy and stops it from drying out during cooking. This is why people often make a marinade for meat before they barbecue it on a hot grill.

For 4 people you need:

INGREDIENTS
1 garlic clove
1 lemon
6 free-range skinless chicken thigh fillets
2 tablespoons olive oil
2 teaspoons honey
1 teaspoon dried oregano

EQUIPMENT
rolling pin ◆ cutting board small paring knife ◆ lemon juicer ◆ mixing bowl spoon ◆ roasting dish oven mitts

1 Bash the garlic clove with a rolling pin – this will help to loosen the pink papery skin – then peel off the skin. Using the rolling pin again, squash the garlic to crush it slightly – this helps its flavour to come out as it cooks. Remember to wash the rolling pin after!

2 Use the bridge-cutting technique to halve the lemon with a small paring knife. Put a lemon half over a lemon juicer and press down to squeeze out the juice. Repeat with the other lemon half.

3 Put the chicken in a mixing bowl and add the garlic, lemon juice, oil, honey and dried oregano. Mix with a spoon, cover and put in the fridge for at least 1 hour. After 1 hour, turn the oven on to 190°C (375°F) Gas 5. Spoon the chicken into a roasting dish (leave the marinade behind). Using oven mitts, put the dish in the oven and roast for 25–30 minutes – ask an adult to help you check if it is cooked. Turn the chicken once during this time. Cut the chicken into small pieces to serve.

SKILLS
◆ BASHING GARLIC
◆ CUTTING
◆ MAKING MARINADE
◆ SQUEEZING LEMONS
◆ USING OVEN

STAGE
3

toffee apple tarts

These tarts are so enjoyable to make that the boys who came over to my house to make them for this book asked to make some more in between taking the photos. Once you know how to make pastry dough, you can make so many different pies, cheese straws, small tarts, big tarts and lots more.

1 Use a table knife to cut the butter into small pieces and put into a mixing bowl with the flour. Rub the butter into the flour with your fingers until it looks like fine breadcrumbs. This can take a few minutes.

2 Add the sugar, egg yolk and water and stir the mixture together with the table knife until it comes together and you can form a ball with your hands. Wrap the pastry in clingfilm/plastic wrap and put it in the fridge for 30 minutes this will make it easier to roll out.

3 Turn the oven on to 180°C (350°F) Gas 4. Using a scrap of parchment paper, rub a little butter inside the holes in the cupcake tins/pans. Break the dough into 4 pieces. Sprinkle a little flour on the work surface, then roll out one piece at a time. Dip the cutter in flour, then cut out 24 circles. Gently press the circles into the holes of the pans.

4 Use the table knife and a cutting board to cut the apples in small pieces, avoiding the core in the middle. Divide the pieces between the pastry cases/dough crusts.

5 Put the toffees on a solid work surface and GENTLY bash with the rolling pin to break into pieces. Scatter the pieces evenly over the apples. Using oven mitts, put the pans in the oven and bake for 15 minutes, or until the toffee has melted and the apples are cooked.

To make 24 little tarts you need:

SWEET PASTRY/PIE CRUST DOUGH
115 g/1 stick unsalted butter, chilled
225 g/1¾ cups plain/all-purpose flour
1 teaspoon sugar
1 egg yolk (see page 84 for separating eggs)
1–2 tablespoons cold water

FILLING
about 6–8 eating apples
12 hard toffee sweets/candies

EQUIPMENT
*table knife • mixing bowl • clingfilm/plastic wrap
parchment paper • 2 x 12-hole cupcake tins/pans
rolling pin • round cutter about 8 cm/3 inches
across • cutting board • oven mitts*

SKILLS
◆ CUTTING
◆ RUBBING BUTTER INTO FLOUR
◆ LINING TART TINS/PANS
◆ SHARING FILLINGS
◆ BASHING WITH ROLLING PIN
◆ USING OVEN

STAGE
3

scones & jam

Once you know how to make scones, you will always have something for tea or for your packed lunches. Why not treat Mum and Dad and make them a batch at the weekend? Lola's friend Annabelle tested this recipe for me and made them once after breakfast and before school for her and her brother's packed lunches! Well done Annabelle!

To make 8–10 scones you need:

INGREDIENTS
225 g/1¾ cups self-raising/ rising flour
1 teaspoon baking powder
40 g/2½ tablespoons unsalted butter, chilled
1 tablespoon sugar
140–150 ml/⅔ cup milk plus a little extra
strawberry jam, to serve

EQUIPMENT
scissors • parchment paper
baking tray • mixing bowl
table knife • round fluted cutter
about 6 cm/2¼ inches across
pastry brush • oven mitts

1 Turn the oven on to 220°C (425°F) Gas 7. Cut a piece of parchment paper big enough to cover the baking tray. Put the flour and baking powder into a mixing bowl. Use a table knife to cut the butter into small pieces and put into the mixing bowl with the flour. Rub the butter into the flour with your fingers until it looks like fine breadcrumbs. This can take a few minutes, so be patient and keep going!

2 Add the sugar and milk. Use a table knife to stir and start to mix everything together.

3 Now use your hands to bring the mixture together to make a ball of dough.

4 Sprinkle a little flour on the work surface, then tip the dough out of the bowl. Pat it gently to flatten until it is about 1.5 cm/⅝ inch thick. Dip the cutter in flour, then cut out scones from the dough. Put the scones onto the baking tray, spaced a little apart. Gather all the spare bits of dough together, roll together to make a ball and flatten out again. Cut out the rest of the scones – you should be able to make 8, 9 or 10 scones depending on the size of your cutter.

5 Dip a pastry brush into a little milk and brush over the scones. Using oven mitts, put the scones in the oven and bake for 10 minutes until risen and golden.

Let cool slightly before cutting in half and serving with strawberry jam and cream, if you like it.

Other good things to add to scones: For fruit scones stir in 50 g/½ cup dried fruit, such as raisins or currants or chopped dried apple or apricots, when you add the sugar. Try adding a pinch of mixed spice/apple pie spice or cinnamon. For cheesy scones, leave out the sugar and stir in 50 g/½ cup grated hard cheese and chopped fresh herbs.

SKILLS
◆ RUBBING BUTTER INTO FLOUR
◆ CUTTING USING CUTTERS
◆ BRUSHING (MILK) USING PASTRY BRUSH

STAGE
3

roasted fruit

When you bake fruit in the oven, the key is to not overcook it otherwise it will get too soft. The times will vary depending on the size of the fruit, but 15 minutes is good for large soft fruits like nectarines or peaches. If you choose smaller fruit like plums, cook them for just 10 minutes. Roasted fruits are great served with plain yogurt. For a treat, add half a teaspoon of thick cream to each fruit half before baking so that you have a sauce at the end of the cooking time.

For 4 people you need:

INGREDIENTS
4 peaches or nectarines, or 8 plums or apricots
3 tablespoons light brown sugar
capful almond or vanilla extract
30 g/2 tablespoons unsalted butter

EQUIPMENT
cutting board • small paring knife • spoon ovenproof dish • oven mitts

1 Turn the oven on to 190°C (375°F) Gas 5. Use the bridge-cutting technique to cut the fruit in half: on a cutting board, make a 'bridge' with a thumb and finger of one hand and hold the fruit. Hold a small paring knife in your other hand and put the blade under the bridge, then cut downwards firmly. You will need to move the fruit around as you cut to avoid cutting through the stone. This will take a bit of time, patience and practice.

2 Use a teaspoon to scoop the stones out of the middle of the fruit. You might need to dig the spoon under the stone to take it out.

3 Rest the fruit in an ovenproof dish with the cut side facing up. Spoon the sugar evenly over each fruit half, add the almond extract and dot with little pieces of the butter. Using oven mitts, put the dish in the oven and bake for 15–20 minutes. I think these peaches look so beautiful, don't you?

SKILLS
◆ CUTTING
◆ CORING/PITTING FRUIT
◆ USING OVEN

STAGE
3

magic citrus desserts

These desserts are light and fluffy on top, with a pool of lemon sauce at the bottom. They are delicate because of the egg white, and that's why they need to be cooked in a roasting dish with water around them to help them cook slowly.

For 4–5 people you need:

INGREDIENTS

1 unwaxed lemon and 1 unwaxed lime (or just 2 lemons or limes, if you like)
100 g/½ cup golden caster sugar/natural cane sugar
50 g/3½ tablespoons unsalted butter, soft
2 free-range eggs
75 g/½ cup plus 1 tablespoon self-raising/rising flour
250 ml/1 cup milk

EQUIPMENT

small grater ◆ mixing bowl ◆ wooden spoon saucer ◆ 2 bowls ◆ balloon whisk ◆ small paring knife ◆ electric mixer ◆ metal spoon 4–5 small pudding basins ◆ deep roasting tin/pan ◆ small jug/pitcher ◆ oven mitts

1 Turn the oven on to 180°C (350°F) Gas 4. Using a small grater, grate the lemon and lime to make zest (see page 60 for how to do this) and put into a mixing bowl. Add the sugar and butter and mix well with a wooden spoon until it becomes fluffy and paler in colour. Crack an egg onto a saucer (see page 60 for how to do this), rest a small bowl over the yolk and tip the white into a clean bowl*. Add the egg yolk to the butter mixture in the mixing bowl and then repeat with the other egg.
2 Add the flour to the mixing bowl and, using a balloon whisk, mix together. Use the bridge-cutting technique to halve the zested lemon with a small paring knife. Squeeze the juice into the mixing bowl, add the milk and whisk.
3 Using a clean balloon whisk or an electric mixer (with help from an adult), whisk the eggs whites in their bowl until they are thick, white and make slight peaks.

5

◆ GRATING
◆ SEPARATING EGGS
◆ FOLDING
◆ WHISKING EGG WHITES

4 Using a metal spoon, 'fold' the egg whites into the batter in the mixing bowl. 'Folding' means to carefully cut the batter and mix without beating all the air out of the egg whites. Fold until the whites are just mixed in.

5 Rub a little butter inside 4–5 small pudding basins and put them in a deep roasting tin/pan. Spoon the batter into the basins, then pour water from a small jug/pitcher into the roasting tin to come halfway up the sides of the basins. Ask an adult to help you put the tin in the oven using oven mitts. Bake for 35 minutes, or until the desserts are golden and cooked with a small pool of sauce in the bottom.

* Did you know that the bowl for egg whites needs to be really clean, or you may not end up with fluffy egg whites?

STAGE
3

blackberry pudding

This is as easy as 1, 2, 3. Measure the ingredients, mix them together and then bake. I have chosen to use ground almonds and single/light cream in this recipe for a really special dessert. However, if you don't have ground almonds you could use self-raising/rising flour and instead of cream you can use milk. It will not have the same flavour or texture, but it's still a nice dessert. You could also try to make this dessert with other fruits that are in season e.g. soft fruits like raspberries, sliced fresh peaches, plum halves or apricot halves, or mixed fruit like raspberries mixed with redcurrants and blackcurrants.

For 4 people you need:

INGREDIENTS
40 g/2½ tablespoons unsalted butter
3 free-range eggs
80 g/a scant ½ cup golden caster sugar/natural cane sugar
capful vanilla extract
150 ml/⅔ cup single/light cream
100 g/1 cup ground almonds
350 g/2 baskets blackberries
a little sugar for the top

EQUIPMENT
parchment paper • medium ovenproof dish • small saucepan • table knife jug/pitcher • fork • oven mitt

1 Turn the oven on to 180°C (350°F) Gas 4. Using a scrap of parchment paper, rub a little butter inside the ovenproof dish. Put the butter in a small saucepan over low heat on the hob/stovetop and heat gently until it has melted. Crack the eggs into a jug/pitcher (see page 60 for how to do this) and measure all the other ingredients.
2 Add the melted butter, sugar, vanilla extract, cream and ground almonds to the eggs in the jug/pitcher and mix together with a fork. Pour this batter into your ovenproof dish.
3 Dot the blackberries all over the batter. Using oven mitts, put the dish into the oven and bake for 30–35 minutes or until the pudding is cooked all the way through. It tastes great with ice cream or yogurt or on its own!

SKILLS
◆ MELTING BUTTER
◆ MIXING
◆ MEASURING
◆ USING OVEN

STAGE
3

Ella's raspberry & white chocolate cake

Ella is the queen of sponge cakes in our house and this cake is based on the classic Victoria sponge cake – named after the queen herself! It was Ella's idea to add fresh raspberries to the batter and to make some lovely big white chocolate buttons for the top. I hope you enjoy making it as much she did!

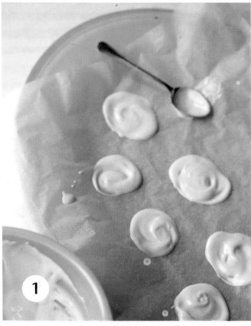

To make 1 big cake you need:

CAKE BASE
100 g/3½ oz. white chocolate
225 g/almost 2 sticks unsalted butter, soft
225 g/1 generous cup golden caster sugar/natural cane sugar
capful vanilla extract
4 eggs, at room temperature
225 g/1¾ cups self-raising/rising flour
400 g/14 oz. ripe raspberries (or fruits of the forest) plus extra to decorate
1 teaspoon baking powder
4 tablespoons raspberry jam

BUTTERCREAM
100 g/6½ tablespoons unsalted butter, soft
150 g/1 cup icing/confectioners' sugar
3 ripe raspberries

ICING
3 ripe raspberries
250 g/2 cups icing/confectioners' sugar
a little water

EQUIPMENT
2 plates ◆ parchment paper ◆ small saucepan
small heatproof bowl ◆ oven mitts ◆ spoon
2 x 20-cm/8-inch cake tins/pans ◆ pencil
scissors ◆ 3 mixing bowls ◆ wooden spoon
table knife ◆ large metal spoon ◆ fork

1 Cover a big plate with parchment paper. Half fill a small saucepan with water and sit a small heatproof bowl in the pan over the water (without the bowl touching the water). Break the chocolate into the small bowl. Put the pan over low heat on the hob/stovetop. When the water starts to heat up, the chocolate will melt. Don't touch the chocolate – leave it until it has melted. Turn the heat off and carefully, using oven mitts, take the bowl off the pan and stir the chocolate. Spoon circles of the chocolate onto the parchment paper and leave somewhere cold to set.

5

6

7

2 Turn the oven on to 180°C (350°F) Gas 4. Using a scrap of parchment paper, rub a little butter inside the cake tins/pans. Rest one tin on some parchment paper and draw around the tin with a pencil. Cut 2 circles out and put in the bottom of the tins.

3 Put the soft butter, sugar and vanilla extract in a mixing bowl and mix well with a wooden spoon until it becomes fluffy and paler in colour. Crack the eggs and add to the batter a little a time, mixing all the time. Add just a little flour, too.

4 Add the raspberries and gently mix together. Don't worry if the batter looks slightly lumpy or curdled —this is normal.

5 Add the flour and, using a large metal spoon, 'fold' it into the batter. 'Folding' means to carefully cut the batter and mix without beating all the air out of it.

6 Spoon the batter equally into the tins/pans. Using oven mitts, put

the tins in the oven and bake for 20 minutes, or until the cakes are well risen and cooked through.

7 Using the oven mitts, take the cakes out of the oven. Let cool, then turn them out of the tins/pans and peel the paper off. To make the buttercream, put the butter, sugar and raspberries in a bowl and mix until really smooth. Put one of the cakes onto a plate and spread the jam over it. Spread the buttercream over the jam and put the other cake on top. To make the icing, mash the raspberries in a bowl with a fork, add the sugar and a little water and mix together. Spoon onto the cake and decorate with more raspberries and the white chocolate buttons.

SKILLS

MEASURING ♦ CREAMING BUTTER & SUGAR ♦ CRACKING EGGS ♦ FOLDING FLOUR SPREADING ♦ MELTING CHOCOLATE

STAGE 3

pick 'n' mix hot choc

For a really special hot chocolate, you can just melt chocolate into milk like Ella is doing here and then add flavour from orange zest or a spice. Otherwise, you can use sweetened cocoa mix. This is a great recipe for making when you have friends over. You can create your own 'drinks bar' with little bowls of spices or orange zest for flavour, and sweets/candies and chocolates for the top. Your friends are likely to have great fun choosing what to add to their hot chocolates.

To make 1 hot chocolate you need:

HOT CHOCOLATE

milk

a few squares milk chocolate or 2 teaspoons sweetened cocoa mix

FLAVOURING

freshly grated ginger, ground cinnamon, grated orange zest

TOPPING

whipped cream in a can (or whipped double/heavy cream)

a selection of sweets/candies e.g. white or milk chocolate buttons, mini-marshmallows, chocolate flakes, sprinkles

EQUIPMENT

cup • small saucepan wooden spoon • spoon

1 Measure the milk in the cup you will be using – pour the milk into your cup and then pour this milk into a small saucepan. Only three-quarters fill your cup, as you will need room for the toppings!

2 Add the chocolate to the pan and heat until it melts and the milk just starts to bubble – don't leave it too long otherwise the milk will rise up inside the pan and spill over the top! Take the pan off the heat. Stir with a wooden spoon until the chocolate has melted.

3 Pour the hot chocolate into your cup.

4 Now decide which flavour you would like to add to your hot chocolate – freshly grated ginger, ground cinnamon and grated orange zest are all good – and stir it in. Top the hot chocolate with whipped cream and chocolates and sprinkles. My children like to add a flake too!

SKILLS

MEASURING • POURING • GRATING

4

index

conversion chart

Weights and measures have been rounded up or down slightly to make measuring easier.

Measuring butter:
A US stick of butter weighs 4 oz. which is approximately 115 g or 8 tablespoons.

American	Metric	Imperial
6 tbsp	85 g	3 oz.
7 tbsp	100 g	3½ oz.
1 stick	115 g	4 oz.

The recipes in this book require the following conversions:

Volume equivalents:

American	Metric	Imperial
1 teaspoon	5 ml	
1 tablespoon	15 ml	
¼ cup	60 ml	2 fl. oz.
⅓ cup	75 ml	2½ fl. oz.
½ cup	125 ml	4 fl. oz.
⅔ cup	150 ml	5 fl. oz. (¼ pint)
¾ cup	175 ml	6 fl. oz.
1 cup	250 ml	8 fl. oz.

Weight equivalents:

Imperial	Metric
1 oz.	30 g
2 oz.	55 g
3 oz.	85 g
3½ oz.	100 g
4 oz.	115 g
6 oz.	175 g
8 oz. (½ lb.)	225 g
9 oz.	250 g
10 oz.	280 g
12 oz.	350 g
13 oz.	375 g
14 oz.	400 g
15 oz.	425 g
16 oz. (1 lb.)	450 g

Measurements:

Inches	cm
¼ inch	5 mm
½ inch	1 cm
1 inch	2.5 cm
2 inches	5 cm
3 inches	7 cm
4 inches	10 cm
5 inches	12 cm
6 inches	15 cm
7 inches	18 cm
8 inches	20 cm
9 inches	23 cm
10 inches	25 cm
11 inches	28 cm
12 inches	30 cm

Oven temperatures:

120°C	(250°F)	Gas ½
140°C	(275°F)	Gas 1
150°C	(300°F)	Gas 2
170°C	(325°F)	Gas 3
180°C	(350°F)	Gas 4
190°C	(375°F)	Gas 5
200°C	(400°F)	Gas 6
220°C	(425°F)	Gas 7

acknowledgements

Thank you so much Vicki, Alison and Leslie for making this book possible; I loved writing it! Vicki, I am particularly excited that your lovely Lara is in some of the photos.

Ella, Lola and Finley, thank you for your ideas and for being such a source of constant inspiration to me. I love you loads. Thanks, too, to David, Mavis, Dad, Liz, Tash and James.

Thank you Susan for the gorgeous photographs. I am so excited that this is your first cookbook and that your children are in it. Iona, thanks for all your help and your great design. Brenda and Esther, we couldn't have done the shoots without your help – thank you both. Céline, thank you once again – I really admire your attention to detail. Jo, you may have been in the background but thank you for your help.

Thanks, too, to Jess and the gorgeous children in the book – Ella, Lola & Finley; Ishbel & Sholto;

Aisha; Amy; Bea & Frankie; Hector, Bob & Betty, Emily; Hannah & Maya; Lara; Mickey; Molly & Oscar; Pia & Isabelle; Sadie; Sam; Thomas. On that note, a big thank you to Mr Elliot, Southover School's fantastic Head Teacher.

Thank you to Anita McCormac, OBE, Director of Focus on Food Campaign, for your help and support. I think the Campaign is amazing and I truly admire all the work you are doing to help the next generation to select, prepare and cook healthy food.

A huge thank you to Penelope Leach. I was utterly thrilled when you agreed to read parts of this book; thank you for your constructive feedback and your quote. I feel honoured.

Marguerite, it was the highlight of my career to have a chat with you at your home. I think you are an inspiration and your quote in my book is like the icing on the cake.